"Looking at consulting from the client's point of view is what you'd expect from a marketing professional, and in *Rasputin For Hire* Goodman does just that. All consultants need to understand the 'make-or-break' importance of marketing to succeed — even if they're not marketers by training."

Juan Negroni — TheJobStressCoach.com
The Conference Board, IMC, ACP, NSA

* * * * *

"The Rasputin connection is brilliant! And every one of the 26 lessons from Rasputin is right on in today's consulting environment."

Vern Nielsen, EVP, Crossflux Inc.

* * * * *

"A comprehensive and practical guide to consulting, *Rasputin For Hire* is a must-read for anyone considering consulting temporarily or as a profession. Great guide for your professional development library."

Julie Jansen, Consultant, Coach, and Author of
I Don't Know What I Want, But I Know It's Not This

* * * * *

"For anyone considering a career as a management consultant, *Rasputin For Hire* offers a practical framework for creating a successful practice – and plenty of tips for seasoned consultants."

Frank Kuchinski, CMC - Secretary
Institute of Management Consultants
Connecticut/Westchester Chapter

Also by Michael A. Goodman

THE POTATO CHIP DIFFERENCE

**How to apply leading edge marketing strategies
to landing the job you want**

RASPUTIN
FOR HIRE

To Ted —
Thank you for your
contributions to this
book — and for
being a great friend
over the years.

Michael A. Godman
11/1/03

RASPUTIN
FOR HIRE

AN INSIDE LOOK AT MANAGEMENT CONSULTING
BETWEEN JOBS OR AS A SECOND CAREER

MICHAEL A GOODMAN

Dialogue Press
Westport, Connecticut

Dialogue Press
P.O. Box 657
Westport, CT 06881-0657

Copyright © 2004 by Michael A. Goodman

ISBN: 0-9702088-1-2
LCCN: 2003094849

Careers > Career Strategy > Management Consulting

www.RasputinForHire.com

Contents

Foreword

man´•age•ment con•sult´•ant *noun* a person
who gives professional or expert advice to those
controlling or directing an institution, organization,
or business enterprise

For the last 20 years or so, I've been filling out forms that ask my occupation with the phrase "management consultant." I'm never quite sure what people are going to do with that information, but they ask so I answer. And I've never really thought much about management consulting as a profession or career until recently. I didn't understand it very well when I began, and over the years I've been too busy "being one" to stop and figure out what it means.

It's interesting that the vast majority of professional management consultants didn't start out with "management consulting" as their career objective. In fact, most people who go into management consulting right out of school do so as a way of gaining exposure to various businesses so they can find and land a line management job, become a client, and hire consultants.

And, if we're to believe the statistics, that's exactly what happens to the vast majority of entry-level people at leading

7

management consulting firms. Those who don't follow this path either burn out from the stress of hard work, long hours, extensive travel, and relentless pressure to perform, or they somehow learn to take the lifestyle in stride and become senior-level consultants, selling larger and more important projects, managing the efforts of all the new entry-level people, and thinking grand thoughts about the nature of business, or the economy, or the latest management theories. Some even find time to write books about their experience.

Clearly it's the rare individual who spends an entire career as a consultant.

More often, management consultants are people who have put in their time at traditional corporate jobs, learned the skills of their functional specialties – marketing, sales, finance, operations, logistics, IT, human resources, perhaps even general management – and then decided to market those skills as independent contractors. Often they work alone – the so-called "lone wolf" consultants – or in small groups, with a shared office and support staff. Occasionally they even open multiple offices and share client responsibilities across a range of specialties or sub-specialties, though that usually occurs after a few years of "solo" consulting.

The thing that makes them all the same is the very thing that defines what they do: they give professional or expert advice to those responsible for running an organization or business.

The idea for this book began a few months after I wrote *The Potato Chip Difference: How to apply leading edge marketing strategies to landing the job you want.* That book deals with applying the same approach to job search and career planning that professional management consultants use with their corporate clients. When I spoke to job seekers about the philosophy in that book, they'd often ask whether I think consulting is a viable strategy for finding the next job, or whether consulting might be a better route to follow than trying to finding the perfect corporate job.

Of course, I always avoided answering those questions. In part that is because career decisions are so personal and individual that there is no single answer that applies to everyone. It's also because I hadn't really thought very hard about consulting as a career path or a business. I'd simply "done it" and enjoyed the rewards, managed the drawbacks, and repeated the process year in and year out.

After I'd ducked the question several dozen times it occurred to me that maybe the issue was important enough to warrant researching, collecting expert opinions, organizing and reporting my own learning and experience, and putting it all down on paper in a book on the subject.

That's how this book was born.

Much of what's in here can also be found buried in "how to" books on consulting. Most of those books, however, are as much devoted to the mechanics of setting up and running a small service business as they are to the real work of consulting, and to the critically important decision-making process that you will have to go through before you make the leap into the deep end of the consulting pool.

This book is targeted very specifically at people who are considering consulting as a second career or as an interim activity while they're between jobs – "in transition," as they say. If that's you, then read on. This book is written for you. When you finish, I promise, the issues will be clear and the decision to consult or not will be much easier for you – maybe even automatic and obvious. That's certainly my objective.

And if you do decide that consulting is right for you, you'll find enough tips, suggestions, and consulting philosophy in these pages to save you from years of trial and error in your newly chosen profession. I've even distilled a lot of what professional consultants have learned into the "5 keys to consulting success" that can make or break a new management consultant.

At the end of this book – in Appendix E – I've included transcripts of interviews with others who have walked this path before. Some made the right decision for themselves and are still consulting. Others learned the hard way that it was not the best lifestyle or career move for them and went back to "real" jobs on the client side. And still others considered consulting as a short-term detour on their climb to the top of the executive ladder, and effectively used their experience as consultants to become better prepared for senior roles in Corporate America.

I've tried in the interviews and case studies in this book to include examples from a broad range of functional and industry applications, and to consider as many different personal situations as possible. Unfortunately, I can't anticipate every special need, and I have probably over-represented the kind of consulting I do myself – marketing strategy and business planning. Maybe that's not so bad, because you can use much of what I include as a basis for planning the marketing strategy for *your* consulting business, if you decide consulting is right for you.

In writing this book I've also adopted a convention of referring to unnamed/gender-neutral clients and consultants with masculine pronouns – "he" or "him" – rather than referring to "he/she" or "him/her." Of course, when an individual in an example is female, I use the appropriate feminine reference. Please don't take this as a form of gender bias; that's not the reason I've made this decision. I simply want the text to be easy reading for everyone, and I think most of us find the "he-slash-she" construction more disruptive than its surface political-correctness would warrant.

Finally, I want to thank all the people who provided valuable input and support in the creation of this book. Some are long-time friends or co-workers; others were recruited specifically because they had input or information that made this book a richer, more helpful resource; still others helped make everything more readable, more interesting, or easier to follow and understand. I truly appreciate all of your contributions.

In particular, thanks (alphabetically) to Jenny Bevins, Ted Cutler, Mose Hasu, Steve Lehman, Mary Ann Noyer, Tom O'Neal, Les Raffel, John Swartley, and Barry Tarshis.

Special thanks to two others: Barry Liss, a longtime friend now living in Australia, who not only provided important input and insights, but also agreed to read and comment on several early drafts of the manuscript; and Brian Goodman, my technical advisor, graphic design consultant, wonderful friend, and son.

Special mention is due to my consulting partner, mentor, and friend, Rich Gold. He taught me a lot about consulting through example, and he is a large part of the reason I have enjoyed a rewarding second career in this profession.

There were many others along the way – clients, friends, fellow crossword puzzle addicts, and even friends-of-friends – who encouraged me and/or played an indirect role in the creation of this book, and I value their contributions too.

Several of the contributors asked to remain anonymous, and I respect their wishes. That doesn't mean their contributions are any less appreciated; only that they proffered them with the express understanding that their names would not be disclosed.

Finally, thanks to my son Jason and to Connie, my soul-mate and life-partner, whose encouragement and patience were instrumental in making this book happen.

Without your support this would have been an impossible task. Thank you.

Michael A. Goodman
Westport, Connecticut

Introduction

This book is all about management consulting. If you bought it because you wanted an authoritative text on Russian history, please return the book now and save yourself from a great disappointment.

Furthermore, the kind of management consulting we're talking about is more strategic, business-focused and general management oriented than technical or specific to any single area of functional expertise. While much of the discussion will apply to more technical and specific functional kinds of consulting, the real emphasis will be on general management consulting – the industry so often characterized as providing outside expertise to tackle long-range strategic planning projects or to create new businesses, policies, and approaches to the market.

Many executives – maybe even most executives – consider consulting at some point in their professional careers. Either they fantasize about how much easier life would be if they could deal exclusively with big picture issues and not have to worry about day-to-day implementation, or they see consulting as an alternative second career – one that is clearly better than a forced early retirement and one that can be pursued while still leaving ample opportunity for golf, tennis, and long walks along the beach.

Despite the popularity of the concept, however, consulting has a lousy reputation. Consulting is often what people say they're doing when they're really out of work, and "out of work" is a growing and serious condition for many executives right now.

Furthermore, there's a recent phenomenon – no doubt encouraged, if not enabled, by the magic of Internet connectivity and a new level of mobility among well-educated, professional corporate executives – that has encouraged people to consider consulting as a viable option to include as part of a job search strategy.

The result, not surprisingly, is that there are more "consultants" looking for meaty projects, less basis for differentiation between them, and less respect for a profession that didn't have a whole lot of it previously.

There's a joke that's been around for a while that likens consultants to sea gulls. They fly in, eat your lunch, dump all over you, and fly out. It's not very flattering to consultants, I think you'll agree. But it's funny (if you can call it that) because it resonates at some level with most people – including potential clients.

And when you look at the history of consulting as a profession, it's hard to find many success stories or case studies that today's consultants might use as a guide. The consultant's work is usually in the background; the client gets the credit for a project well done. And when the consultant screws up, it's often an occasion for more consultant jokes, ridicule, and a reinforcement of the already less-than-desirable image. Consultants are right up there with used car salesmen, unscrupulous lawyers, and telemarketers when it comes to their reputation with many in the business community.

So why am I writing a book about consulting and using the infamous Rasputin as a poster child for the profession?

Introduction

The last thing I want to do is set up Grigori Yefimovich Rasputin as a role model or icon for consultants. He was more evil than good, and his life, taken as a whole, is not one any of us should want to emulate.

That said, Rasputin is arguably the best-known consultant in modern history, and he did do many things right when it comes to implementing a successful consulting strategy. (Ultimately his strategy got him killed, so let's not get too excited about how clever he was.) We can learn from Rasputin by imitating what he did well and shunning his less noble actions. Russian history – and Grigori Rasputin in particular – indeed can provide the basis of an excellent tutorial for management consultants today.

In short order, I'll review the fateful period in Russian history from 1904 to 1917 not so much as a history lesson as a case study in establishing a consulting practice – noting both the positive lessons learned and those aspects which, in hindsight, even Rasputin might have changed if he had another chance.

As I do this, I will try to stick to the story of Rasputin as told in the history books, even though they are not in total agreement on every point. I also will tend to focus on those aspects germane to Rasputin's role as a consultant, minimizing discussion of his religious views, rumored sexual exploits, or drinking habits, and steering clear of the complex politics and alliances surrounding European royalty.

For those of you who are legitimate Russian history buffs, I'm afraid you'll be somewhat disappointed in the depth of my own scholarly research. It was never my intent to explain what happened a century ago in Russia or why. I'm simply trying to draw on the experience of a well-known "consultant" to help his modern-day counterparts achieve success in their professional lives.

I also must disclose up-front that my awareness of Rasputin as "Consultant to the Tsar" is not something I came upon entirely on my own. Rather, it is the result of a client's reference to me as "his Rasputin" that sent me to the history books to see if I should be pleased or displeased with the label. Interestingly, though I am certainly not proud to be placed in the same category with a semi-literate, uneducated charlatan, I was forced to admit that there were many appropriate parallels between my role serving that client – a tsar in his own world – and Rasputin's with Tsar Nicholas and Tsarina Alexandra.

I'll be sharing those with you in the pages that follow. My guess is you'll smile as I did when you recognize how much we can learn from "The Evil Monk," as Rasputin was known.

Chapter 1

The Story of a Successful Consultant

Greg didn't have a graduate degree or a resume that was particularly impressive, but he had learned some valuable skills and understood enough about the fundamentals of consulting to achieve what many would consider a stellar level of success in his chosen profession. He'd traveled a bit, seen a number of professionals in action, and he was astute enough to learn from them. He was a quick study, insightful analyst, and effective communicator.

Shortly after returning from one of his trips, Greg found himself out of work, with no money and in need of some cash to fund his next venture. He was also astute enough to recognize that the real key to leveraging his skills was to find an employer who really needed his expertise, and to bill not for his time but for his know-how. He needed to capture the full value of his deliverable to the client, not just rent himself out by the hour or the day. Instead of poring through the classified ads or going door-to-door asking for work, he embarked on an in-depth research project to find a potential employer whose greatest need was precisely what Greg knew how to do best. It took a bit of digging, and a few months of hard work, but he eventually found the situation he knew would be perfect for his needs – the ideal consulting gig, if he could land it.

He developed a strategy that he'd seen work many times before. He began to network with individuals who might know key people at the target client. He was still in research mode, and he learned even more about the client from his contacts. It seemed the client was in over his head. The job was terribly complex, and there were so many pieces to manage that it was impossible to set and stick to priorities. Besides, the client wasn't really cut out for the job to begin with. To make matters worse, the number two person was preoccupied with other matters, and the internal staff simply didn't have the skills or know-how to deal with the seemingly unsolvable problems.

It didn't take long before Greg had an action plan to implement. He secured the introductions he needed. He would "work his magic" to solve Number Two's biggest problem, thus establishing a credential that would earn him the trust and respect of everyone on the client team.

When the time came, it worked just as he'd planned it. Number Two agreed to meet with him based on referrals from his networking contacts. He committed to solving Number Two's biggest single problem, in return for a nice consulting fee and an introduction to the Big Boss. The price he set was high considering the time and effort involved, but quite reasonable considering the benefits for the client. And there didn't seem to be any viable alternative, so he was not really competing on a price basis anyway.

When his proposal was accepted, Greg wasted no time. He got to work and delivered everything he'd promised – and in record time to boot. Everyone on the client team was impressed. Clearly Greg had established his value and earned the right to bid on future projects.

The Story of a Successful Consultant

Of course, there were those on the internal staff who felt threatened. After all, the new consultant had been able to solve a problem that had eluded them, and it was clear that his services would be needed on an ongoing basis. Greg was sensitive to their reaction and tried to befriend and support them as best he could. Nonetheless, he knew his first loyalty was to Number Two; Number Two was confident in giving Greg additional assignments and even introduced him to the Big Boss.

As time passed, Greg continued to deliver high value to his client, though the Big Boss never quite accepted him the way Number Two did. Then Greg got his big break: The Big Boss was reassigned and Number Two moved into the top spot. Greg was right where he wanted to be, making his unique contribution and being well rewarded for the high value he delivered.

The story would end there were it not for growing resentment and hostility among the internal team. They were constantly being compared to the "brilliant consultant" and coming up second best. They had to find a way to remove him or they'd live in his shadow forever. And Greg refused to compromise his own standards of performance or shift his loyalties to win their acceptance. Besides, he'd become accustomed to a pretty nice lifestyle, and he enjoyed as much influence on important matters as an outsider reasonably could expect.

To address its problem, the inside team came up with a plan, arranging to give Greg an important assignment that no consultant possibly could deliver. When he failed, they used it as proof that "the magic was gone" and Greg was back on the street, out of work once again. From a career standpoint, he was finished. No client would hire the high-profile consultant who lost his touch and failed.

If there's poetic justice, it's in the postscript to the story. Within months of Greg's departure, the entire enterprise collapsed and Number Two was out. So was the former Big Boss, and the entire dynasty was history. When the post-mortem was written, much of the blame for failure came to rest on Greg's shoulders, though by that time it didn't matter any more. He'd had a wonderful career, done great things for his client, and been rewarded for the value delivered at the time.

What we can learn from Greg

It should come as no surprise to you at this point that "Greg" is none other than Grigori Yefimovich Rasputin. The Big Boss is Tsar Nicholas II, and Number Two is his wife, the Tsarina Alexandra Feodorovna. Their "enterprise" was the Russian Empire, and all of this took place between 1904, when Alexandra discovered that her infant son and only male heir, Alexis, was a hemophiliac, and the end of the Romanov Dynasty in 1917 – just a few months after Rasputin's untimely death at the hands of the "internal staff" at the Royal Palace.

In fact, Rasputin's first project for Alexandra was to save the life of her bleeding infant son, controlling his hemophilia by some "magic" that to this day remains a mystery. (He repeated the feat more than once, so there must have been something to it.)

In the appendix to this book, I've reproduced one account of the chapter in Russian history that includes a detailed narrative of Nicholas, Alexandra, and "Greg" so that you can see for yourself how closely my paraphrasing of the story parallels the recorded history from the early years of the twentieth century. (It has a lot more detail than would be useful for our purposes, but I know the purists and history majors will appreciate it. There are even a few paragraphs in it that might contain additional insights for new consultants.)

For now, let's go back through Greg's story and identify the lessons for consultants that will be discussed in more detail in the pages that follow. I have found twenty-six important lessons in the first eleven paragraphs describing Greg's experience.

The Story of a Successful Consultant

Paragraph 1:

- Formal education isn't nearly as important as having useful, marketable skills.
- You can learn by observing others, as long as (a) they're the right people, and (b) you know what to watch for/learn from them.
- Critical skills: quick study, insightful analysis, effective communication.

Paragraph 2:

- Key is finding the right client.
- Bill for what you deliver; focus on the benefit, not on how many hours/days it will take you to do the job. (Clients value what they pay for and pay for what they value.)

Paragraph 3:

- Consulting jobs don't find you; you find them.
- It's not a numbers game.
- Research is the most important element in landing a consulting project, and it's all done up-front. (This also applies to a job search, of course.)
- Identify a project that requires what you do best.

Paragraph 4:

- Networking is primarily a research tool.
- Consulting works best when you have skills the client doesn't have.

Paragraph 5:

- Strategic planning comes first; then implementation.
- Consider the client individuals/team, not just the business issues.

Paragraph 6:

- Pre-play all important meetings: "What's the best thing that can happen at this meeting?"
- Keep it simple stupid. (KISS)
- Don't be a commodity.
- Price to value!

Paragraph 7:

- Over-deliver against client expectations – and do it fast.
- Establish your value/expertise as quickly as possible.
- Plan the future relationship as you deliver the initial project.

Paragraph 8:

- Each deliverable should logically tie to the next project.
- Remember who the client is and what success looks like from the client's perspective.

Paragraph 9:

- Always place the client's best interests first.
- Be sure the client feels you're delivering value in excess of your cost.

Paragraph 10:

- Work hard to be accepted by the client team; discuss potential people problems with the client, and include people issues in the project proposal. You'll need to deal with them sooner or later, so better to be candid about them early.

Paragraph 11:

- Never accept an assignment that you don't think you can master. Consulting is a "zero tolerance" business.

In this book I will deal with each of these 26 points by explaining them in more detail and using the principles they represent to answer some key questions that every consultant, and would-be consultant, should ask. I won't necessarily address them in order or identify them explicitly at every point, but will cover them all in the context of contemporary consulting. Also I'll discuss in some detail the basis and rationale for each of the lessons. Then toward the end of the book we'll review Greg's story and see how the lessons all fit together.

A footnote on Rasputin

While history has not treated Grigori Rasputin particularly well, the vast majority of Russian people at the time had a considerably different view of The Evil Monk. Because he was a "holy man" with peasant roots who made it to a position of great influence with the most powerful royalty in all of Europe, Rasputin was something of a folk hero in early twentieth century Russia. He represented hope on the part of the Russian people that the tsars would never forget the plight of the common man. And when he was assassinated at the hands of aristocrats, and even members of the imperial family, the upper classes lost whatever support they might have had from the inhabitants of their estates. Indeed, the Russian empire collapsed in a matter of weeks after Rasputin's death.

The romantic in me would like to think that outside consultants who help their client companies improve the quality of their businesses will be appreciated by the stockholders and employees – much as Rasputin was by the Russian peasants – even if the managers who hired them take all the credit and quickly forget the consultants' contributions, or are no longer in a position to make a real difference themselves.

I know better, but I'm sure you can understand this consultant's fantasy!

Chapter 2

Consulting Between Jobs
or as a Second Career

This book was created very specifically to help you decide if consulting is something that makes sense for you. Whether you're thinking about consulting while you're in transition (i.e., between jobs) or as a possible second career, you need to know what you're getting into and to be able to project what your life will be like after you take the plunge.

To accomplish that objective, I've looked at consulting in a number of ways – each covered in one of the chapters of this book.

First I look at what consulting really is – the essence of consulting. I compare it to some closely-related activities and define the core deliverables of a consultant. To make sure there is no misunderstanding, I also discuss a few tools and characteristics that help to describe what it is that consultants really do.

Then I get right into the key factors you'll need to take into account if consulting looks attractive to you at first glance. I go through the seven important prerequisites for becoming a successful consultant, explain how I was able to capture the essence of my own unique positioning in a Mission Statement for my consulting firm, and discuss some of the lifestyle, business, and personal issues that you'll want to consider as you analyze your own situation.

Next, I look at a typical consulting project – all nine phases – so that you get a chance actually to live through the cycle that repeats itself over the course of a consultant's career. Short of becoming a consultant, this is probably as close as you can get to understanding what your life will be like should you decide to consult.

Then I examine a typical consulting proposal – not so much as the template for a document, but as a surrogate for the way you'll live your life as a consultant. Think of the proposal as the contract you'll sign to deliver valuable services and recommendations to your client in return for pre-agreed compensation. If you think you can thrive under the terms of the contract, you're probably going to be a pretty good consultant. Incidentally, there's a sample proposal in Appendix B, near the end of this book, that demonstrates how the principles covered in the discussion actually look when they get into a document that goes to the client.

The two chapters after that look at consulting from the client's point of view. It's not always easy to see yourself objectively – let alone through your customer's eyes – so I thought it would be instructive to present that alternate perspective before you make your decision. The first of these chapters considers what a client is looking for and why they might hire a consultant. The second looks at the five most widely held misconceptions, or myths, clients have about consultants in my own field – marketing and strategic planning. It won't take you long to extend the thinking into your own area of expertise, and you may be able to pick up some pointers that will prove useful in marketing your services as a consultant.

In Chapter 9, I talk specifically about consulting when you're between jobs. Most of the considerations are the same as if you were embarking on a second career in consulting, with the main difference being that you don't plan to stay there very long. I examine the pros and cons, offer some thoughts on how to make that decision, and suggest an alternative should you decide that consulting is not something you want as part of your job search strategy.

By the time you get to Chapter 10, you should have a pretty good idea of whether consulting is right for you. That's where I share the five keys to consulting success. After all, if you're going to join the ranks of consulting professionals you'll want to know exactly what it takes to be successful. After you read this chapter, and perhaps re-read it, you may also want to review the notes on Positioning which I include in Appendix C. You'll want to start your consulting excursion by creating a Positioning Statement for your business/ yourself – an important first step that's not to be taken lightly.

I also discuss the importance of ethical behavior as a consultant. There are more "gray areas" than most of us realize before we enter consulting, and it's important that you be sensitive to them – not just because you want to be seen as an honest, upright citizen and highly-principled consultant, but also because it can have a direct impact on your business and on your immediate decision to become a consultant or not. In Exhibit D, I've included a Code of Ethics developed by the Institute of Management Consultants. It includes all the right considerations, and it captures, I think, the essence of what constitutes ethical behavior on the part of a management consultant.

Finally, in the last chapter, we'll revisit the twenty-six lessons we listed from Greg's experience at the beginning of this book, and recap the key learnings from Rasputin – all of which are covered in the pages between.

In the course of putting this all together, I've had the benefit of input from a range of people with experience in different kinds of consulting, different functional specialties, and different reactions to their consulting experiences. I learned a lot from my interaction with them and I think you might enjoy and benefit from some of their specific comments as well. I've included an edited and simplified transcript of our discussions in Appendix E. You shouldn't be surprised that many of their thoughts and insights are sprinkled throughout the book. What the transcript adds, I think, is a "human" and personal context for many of the observations and conclusions.

Chapter 3

The Essence of Consulting

Before we get into a discussion of whether consulting is a good between-jobs strategy or an attractive second career option, I think it's important to clarify what we mean by consulting. New consultants sometimes equate being a contract employee or a consultative sales representative with being a consultant, and that's not really the subject here.

Of course, consultants usually *are* contract employees, but the overwhelming majority of contract employees are most definitely NOT consultants. The distinction is very relevant to the discussion at hand.

Consultants provide advice, insight, unique knowledge, know-how, creative services, or other intellectual property as their primary deliverable. They do NOT primarily sell or rent their time and presence, or perform routine tasks according to pre-determined procedures.

A temporary data entry person may be a contract employee, but he or she wouldn't be considered a consultant. Similarly, a part-time night manager at the local convenience store might be a contract employee, but he or she wouldn't be a consultant.

By way of contrast, a company might hire a consultant to establish the procedures or job descriptions for temporary data entry people or to determine whether it makes good business sense to hire part-time night managers at a group of convenience stores.

The distinction is that consultants provide advice, develop policies and procedures, or deliver a creative product, while other contract employees provide a service that requires their physical presence or time.

Additionally, when we use the term "deliverable" for a consultant, we mean the end-product that the consultant must generate and "deliver" to the client in order to fulfill his part of the consulting contract or agreement. The deliverable always includes the substance of what the consultant must do or produce; it also usually includes the format for acceptable delivery.

In some cases the form of the deliverable might be fully-debugged and executable computer code that performs pre-agreed functionality. In other cases it might take the form of a written report that includes an executive summary, detailed discussion of key issues, and exhibits with detailed tables, graphs, and other supporting data that provide the rationale for a consultant's recommendations. Or the deliverable might simply take the form of a meeting at which the consultant presents findings, conclusions, creative content, and/or recommendations to the client management team. All of these are examples of the format of a consultant's "deliverables."

Don't confuse the format with the substance. The substance is the essence. The format is just the "package." You wouldn't confuse a letter with the envelope in which it came, would you? Similarly, you wouldn't confuse the message or meaning of a letter with the letter itself. What the consultant "delivers" physically might be a thick, bound, written report; that's the format. But the content – the actual recommendation or creative product – is the real deliverable, without which the report would be just a lot of wasted paper in a three-ring binder.

Notice that in drawing the distinction between consultants and other contract employees I haven't mentioned the compensation, duration of assignment, or specific terms of engagement. I'm also not suggesting that consulting is somehow superior to other kinds of contract employment. The distinction is strictly one of the primary deliverable. Consultants don't primarily deliver hours or days; they deliver advice, sound thinking, solutions to problems, novel approaches, or other creative services. The fact that they might have to spend time or show up to do their jobs is incidental to their primary deliverable. And the format of the deliverable is simply the package, or "envelope," they use to convey the deliverable, not the deliverable itself.

Think about Rasputin and his "consulting deliverable." His first assignment was to stop the bleeding of a child with hemophilia. There was no requirement that he spend hours or days on the job, produce a detailed report on his methodology, explain the scientific principles on which his approach was based, or even physically show up on specific occasions. His job was to keep the child from bleeding to death, and he delivered on the project. (It's nice when the deliverable is so clear-cut – pardon the pun – and measurable.)

Subsequent "assignments" for Rasputin were perhaps less well defined, but it's likely the Tsarina sought his advice on how to run the empire, whom to trust, or how to handle specific situations. She wanted his advice and guidance, not simply to have him put in an appearance, show up at the palace a set number of hours or days, create lengthy and detailed reports, or merely keep his office occupied.

Consultative sales

And consulting is different from consultative sales, too. Consultative sales consists of a sales representative's helping his customers genuinely improve their businesses; that's his primary task. In that sense, the sales representative IS a consultant. The theory is that when a sales representative behaves like a true consultant the client will ultimately return the favor, show loyalty to the "consultant" and his company and/or product, and become a bona fide customer.

I'm a big fan of consultative sales because it embodies a truly customer-oriented attitude and because it almost always results in a more satisfactory win-win approach between seller and buyer. The seller's representatives have as their mission to help the buyers improve their businesses, and the buyers, once they understand the game, are motivated to share information that will make the entire transaction better for both parties.

I often wonder why every business doesn't employ a consultative sales approach. But that's not the subject of this book, nor should it be confused with a career in consulting. Consultative salespeople are, in the final analysis, selling something. That's their mission. Consultants, on the contrary, are paid to provide advice, know-how, or creative services – not to directly and immediately stimulate or encourage purchase orders for some other product or service – though it's always nice when you can deliver that outcome as a bonus.

The contemporary consulting proposal

In my own practice now, when we submit a proposal for a consulting project, we typically state the objective(s) of the project, describe and define the deliverables, and discuss the work plan we expect to follow in order to do our jobs. Of course, we are sure to include an estimate of the timetable for each work plan element, milestones, final completion date, fees and payment schedules, expectations for client participation (if any), and any possible "extras" or conditional elements.

We always make it clear, though, that the clients are buying the deliverables, not the work plan. We go to great lengths to position the project in a strategic context and identify the specific benefits the client will realize once the deliverables are in hand. Not only are we "selling" the project, but we want to be sure the client doesn't start counting hours or days for on-site appearances, number of pages in a report, lines of computer code, or calculations and presentations. We want them focused on the core benefits they'll reap from the work we do.

This bit of philosophy will be the subject of more discussion later, when I get into some consulting "how-to" elements. I begin to plant the thought here because I think it helps make the point about what consulting is. It's about the consultant's product, or deliverable, as a form of intellectual property that has value to the client. And it's about what defines consulting and distinguishes it from some close cousins or even sibling careers.

Consultants as psychics or seers

Another preview of our future discussion may be in order now too, as it is relevant to defining what consultants do. Consultants must have knowledge, know-how, or insight that their clients don't possess. We sometimes refer to this as "consulting insight," alluding to a kind of intuitive awareness that is inherent in most of us. Some consultants even allude to their clairvoyance as part of a sales pitch.

Of course, most of us don't flaunt it or pretend to be card-carrying psychics. That's not what it's all about. In fact, many professional consultants deny that they use intuition, or at least explain it as "drawing on extensive experience." And maybe that's exactly what it is. Let's not get into a definition of intuition just yet.

The point of this is that consulting is a career in which the deliverable is an insight, novel solution, or recommendation that has value to the client. It's primarily an intellectual or creative product – not just man-hours or on-site presence.

"Who-do-you-know" consultants

There's a special case of consulting as a second career that bears some mention. It's not exactly consulting as we've defined it, but it's quite common and it's almost always called "consulting," so it makes sense at least to acknowledge it here. It's consulting just after you voluntarily retire from full-time work.

Here's how it goes: A recent retiree isn't fully prepared to shift gears and really retire. He has worked hard all his life and finds it difficult to simply turn off his business thinking and do nothing but play golf. Besides, he has a small army of associates and friends in the industry, company, and functional specialty, and it's nice for everyone to keep in touch with old friends.

So what happens is this: Someone still active in the business needs a contact who can help put a deal together, or find out who is available to fill a position, and they remember the recently retired executive. They call and ask, and the retiree is happy to be of service. They enter a loose "consulting" agreement, and everyone wins. The retired executive has the industry knowledge and contacts, and his old friends need exactly that.

I'd be the last person to discourage this kind of consulting; it's a wonderful way to operate for both the client and the consultant. But it's not the kind of consulting we're dealing with in this book. It's a part-time thing that is more connection-making than creative problem-solving. The fee is usually based on a fair per-diem rate, and the project and deliverable are almost always straightforward and short-term.

I'm not dismissing this as some kind of inferior consulting; I simply point out that it's different from the consulting that people between jobs think about, and it's certainly not a "second career" in the true sense of the phrase.

Consultants as Paid Friends

There's an element of the service consultants provide that some consider almost a personal friendship or allegiance. I've certainly found myself befriending clients more often than not, and I definitely have a loyalty to my clients. I do not, however, think of myself as a "paid friend." That's not what the job is about, even if the friendship is one result.

I see my role more as one of being a partner – teacher, mentor, co-director, stakeholder, etc. – in the client's professional life. I want what's best for the company, and if delivering what's best helps makes the individual client a hero, and gets him promoted or otherwise rewarded, it's some proof that I've done my job well.

I always remain keenly aware that as an outside consultant I'm not a permanent employee, and I have to earn my next project with outstanding performance on the current one. My loyalty is to my own reputation and to the next project, referral, and/or off-hand comment the client may make to a prospective client in the future. If a personal friendship develops, I don't fight it. I just don't think that's a central element in a successful consulting relationship. I've had many projects in which the individual relationships were strictly professional, with only a minimum of what I'd call "personal friendship." Of course, it's always nicer to work with and for people you like.

Chapter 4

Is Consulting Right For You?

Many executive job seekers today consider consulting as an option for their "second career," and even more think about the possibility of including a temporary consulting stint as part of their job search strategy. It is therefore highly relevant to look at the specific issues that need to be included in an assessment of consulting as either a short-term or longer-term career alternative. That's precisely what I'll examine in the next several chapters.

What makes for a good consultant?

Having consulted for almost 25 years now, I think I know the personal requirements for success. Just to be sure, though, I approached half a dozen of my colleagues and solicited their opinions as well. I didn't bias them with my own list; rather, I asked them each to come up with their own, and requested that they not discuss this with each other prior to submitting their thoughts.

I am reassured as a result of the fact that their collective list included all the elements on my own list, and three of the six had lists that were virtually identical to mine. The other three each combined or disaggregated a few items but essentially included all the same thoughts. That should be reassuring to you, as it was to me. It says we're probably on the right track.

Here is the list of the seven personal requirements we all agree are important for an individual to be successful in consulting:

1. You have to understand and love selling
2. You have to like working alone
3. You have to be a quick study
4. You have to be analytical
5. You have to be insightful and/or intuitive
6. You have to be a good communicator
7. You have to have confidence in your own abilities

Of course, we used different words and phrases to explain many of the items on the list, and we ranked them differently in terms of importance, but in the end we were of the same mind when it came to the actual meaning of what was on the list.

Discussion of the prerequisites

Keep in mind, we all presupposed that anyone considering consulting would have the necessary technical or functional skills and experience. I hardly could be a consultant in microbiology or structural engineering, for example, but I do have a wealth of experience in marketing strategy.

You clearly need a background and credentials that clients will find believable and useful as they deal with the issues facing them. You also are responsible for delivering the goods at the end of the day, so it should go without saying that you MUST possess the basic skills, knowledge, and experience. If you don't, the rest of this discussion is meaningless.

With that said, let me share with you some of the discussion and rationale for each of the personal requirements we identified.

You have to understand and love selling

This is the item I knew all the consultants would have near the top of their lists. Most people who are not consultants either don't fully appreciate how important the selling process is, or don't realize how much of a consultant's time and attention it consumes. They are more focused on delivering the project once it's sold, and they forget that there is no project until someone sells it.

The vast majority of consulting assignments are not invented by the client. Clients usually don't figure out that they need a consultant to tackle a tough assignment and then issue an RFP (a "Request For Proposals"). That happens occasionally, of course, but it's not the norm. More often a consultant recognizes the problem a company has and believes he or she can solve that problem better, faster, or more efficiently than the company (or internal staff) could on its own. The consultant then approaches a key decision maker at the company, presents his or her credentials, and writes a consulting proposal to address the problem. The consultants who are better at this "selling" process usually end up with the best and most important assignments.

Furthermore, in many kinds of consulting the selling cycle is quite long – perhaps a year or more between the initial contact and the official approval to begin. We all hope it will be shorter next time, or that we're different and can close the deal faster than the next person, but somehow the lead-time for consulting projects is always a little longer than you think it will, or should, be. That's certainly been my experience, and every one of the consultants with whom I spoke smiled in recognition that this is usually the way it is.

What this means is that each consulting project will be in "selling mode" for months before it moves into implementation. In fact, the duration of the selling cycle is often longer than the project itself. If you don't enjoy this up-front part of the job, you're going to find yourself spending a lot of time at something you don't love.

And the selling process itself has several components. First, the consultant must understand his or her own capabilities; then he must do the research to find a client with a problem he can solve; and finally, he must convince the client to pay the fee to have the problem solved.

Larger projects generally require more time and higher fees, and the decision to commission the project will require more client consideration, management discussion, and longer incubation time prior to reaching a decision to proceed.

When you look at consulting as a business, the selling process is tough: it takes time, lots of research, and effective communication skills just to get in the front door. And, of course, the project has to make economic sense for the client; no manager is going to knowingly spend more to address a problem than the solution is worth.

If the pressure to always be in selling mode is uncomfortable for you, you're probably not going to enjoy consulting very much, and you probably won't be very successful at it. You'll be competing against a lot of folks who enjoy selling and are very good at it.

When we discussed this requirement, many of the consultants with whom I spoke said they might not have gone into consulting at all if they had truly understood the implications of this point up-front. Most of us were lured by the life-style benefits, earning potential, travel opportunities (if you consider that a plus), and fascinating nature of the work. Many of us were also drawn into consulting by a kind of ego satisfaction – the notion that respected, powerful, senior executives would come to us for advice. And a few of us saw consulting as a more lucrative form of teaching, and we see ourselves primarily as teachers.

What we didn't see quite so clearly is the flip side of the coin. You only work when you are successful at selling. And when you're not working, there's no income. When you are working, the pressure to sell the next project is almost as great as the pressure to deliver the current project, because no matter where you are on a project, you know it's going to end at some point, and you'll be out of work (again) if you don't have another one waiting in the wings.

The cycle can become very hectic, and the potential for over-taxing yourself is unlike anything on the client side. If you dedicate yourself to doing a great job for your clients, you don't have enough time to sell. And if you don't make time to sell the next project, you'll be out of work as soon as the current project is over.

You have to like working alone

This is another item I suspected would show up on a lot of lists. Even when consultants work as a team, there's a lot of individual work, and if you're hoping that you can count on your teammates to win the game, you're probably not someone they want on their team. The team is only as strong as its weakest link, and if you're a strong link, you will probably be frustrated by having to compensate for the weaker links.

It's not like a baseball or soccer game where each team member has a different function or assignment, and everyone has to be present to win. In baseball, for example, the pitcher can't very well pitch and play left field, first base and catcher all at the same time. In soccer, you usually can't score a goal if you're the goalie. Each position has a role, and the team only works if each person does his/her job.

In consulting, the client needs (and is paying for) a solution to an important problem. How many people there are on the consulting team isn't important to them, and how you split the workload among the players isn't something they care about. They're looking for the deliverable, and if you're the person who promised it, then YOU are on the line for delivering it.

It's OK to have internal discussions, share the grunt-work, build on each other's ideas, and confer with each other before presenting your solution and recommendations to the client. But most of the time, as Harry Truman so eloquently said, "The buck stops here!" – on *your* desk – and *you* have to be prepared to do whatever it takes to make things work. You're alone in the final analysis.

That's not comfortable for a lot of people. They need and enjoy the social aspects of the workplace, the collaboration, and the camaraderie of a team-working environment. There's nothing wrong with this, but in consulting you are usually not in frequent social contact with the people for and with whom you work. You need to recognize this up front, or you probably won't enjoy consulting very much – and you'll probably be less effective than you'd like. Of course, you can't be a total introvert either. In most cases you'll need to interact with clients and display your professional and social skills on a regular basis. Just don't count on that as an every-day source of psychic, intellectual, or emotional nourishment. In the final analysis, you will mostly be working alone.

You have to be a quick study

This is the component that probably had the greatest variation in how it was expressed, though it was on everyone's list and was considered very important.

Some referred to this requirement as being a "skilled active listener" – really understanding what's on the client's mind, what success looks like for the client, and what the real agenda includes. And this is clearly part of what's required to be a good consultant.

Others think a better way to explain the concept is to look at "intellectual curiosity." When you're naturally interested in learning for the sake of learning you have a better chance of amassing the information that will lead to an innovative and workable solution. That's true too, and most successful consultants have this kind of innate curiosity.

Four of us, though, think the phrase "quick study" best captures the idea. This is different from being intelligent, having a photographic memory, or being a skilled and intense researcher. It has to do with how quickly you are able to understand a situation and grasp the implications. We don't mean to suggest that it isn't important to have a great memory or be a good researcher, but there's more to it than that: you have to be able to do it quickly.

This is also the list component that was, in three cases, combined with the point below on being insightful and/or intuitive.

Clients are often faced with complex situations in industries that have unique requirements, peculiarities, and relationships. They understand things largely as a result of having had to deal with them for years – perhaps having been taught by a mentor when they began – and it's not easy to explain everything to an outsider, at least not quickly.

Even in an industry you know well, each company may have its own slant on things, its unique vocabulary, and its own internal processes and procedures for dealing with the tasks that make up the business. It's hard to explain all of this to the outside consultant quickly. Ideally, the client would like a consultant who already understands, or who can quickly pick up on, the situation and culture without a lengthy (and sometimes painful) start-up period.

All the consultants, myself included, agreed that being a "quick study" is more important in consulting than having specific industry experience. There are certain advantages to bringing an outside perspective, as long as you can bring yourself up to speed before the client realizes you weren't always there.

I've actually landed a couple of projects because I was the outsider and wasn't saddled with "industry baggage," but I had to pick up the nuances of the business and industry quickly, because the client wasn't about to fund a lengthy education process. Other times I've been able to use what I learned on one project to help me "crack the code" on another project with a minimum of new input. From the client's perspective, it looked like I'd picked up on the nuances of his situation almost instantaneously.

Here's an example. I was working in the carbonated soft drink category in the United States. The project was to evaluate an innovative consumer promotion and determine whether it could be redeployed more than once a year, and whether there seemed to be any "wear out" or decreased effectiveness in subsequent uses. ("Do consumers get tired of this promotion, or is it just as interesting and motivating the second or third time around?")

To get at the issue, I visited the markets where the promotion had originally been tested and where it was running for the second or third time. I interviewed sales representatives, aisle clerks, store managers, and the franchise holder's management team in each of those areas. I asked lots of questions and was armed with a book full of sales reports, market share tabulations, and other relevant information.

I learned a lot and was able to give my client useful input that proved accurate – and very profitable. Consumers loved the promotion just as much the second or third time as the first, but the sales team and franchise owners began to think it was a little "tired," and they didn't support the effort with the same enthusiasm as they had when it was really new. Our recommendation was to give them the flexibility to run the promotion as often as they wanted in their markets, with a strong suggestion that they should consider it at least once a year because of the high consumer acceptance and dramatic sales increases. Case closed.

The client followed our recommendation and it worked. Most franchises ran the promotion at least twice a year, and some even ran it three times a year.

Then several years later I had a new assignment with an international not-for-profit organization. It was a membership driven professional association, with chapters all over the world. In fact, more than two-thirds of the members lived outside the United States and the organization was headquartered in both Geneva and Washington, D.C. Now you wouldn't think my soft drink experience would be very useful in that situation, would you?

It proved to be the single most important element in the project, gave me instant credibility with the new client, and proved to be the key to delivering a strategic plan that exceeded the client's expectations.

The project began with a series of visits to and conversations with chapter heads (in Europe and Asia) to learn what they saw as the biggest opportunities and challenges facing the organization.

I recognized very early in the process that the chapter heads in most countries thought and behaved very much like the independent franchise bottlers from my soft drink experience. Despite the symbiotic relationship between headquarters and the field organizations, there was an element of conflict, or tension, that created a "we-they" attitude in both situations.

The field organizations wanted to feel independent, make decisions on their own, and respond to local conditions, while the headquarters staffs saw the chapters and franchise owners more as implementers of plans developed by the central management team. The chapters perceived a kind of arrogance on the part of the headquarters team ("They think they know everything!"), and the headquarters team felt the chapters were too focused on the local issues and missed the bigger picture. ("They think the world revolves around their own problems, and they miss the global importance of what we're trying to accomplish.")

As a result of my "quick study" discovery for the international professional association, I was able to devise a plan that incorporated a great deal of flexibility for the chapters (so they could repeat successful membership programs as often as they wanted to) and still give my headquarters-based clients the overall sense of control they felt they needed. The learnings from a decade earlier, in an industry and situation that exist quite apart, ended up serving me – and my client – very well.

This is just one example of how "quick study" consultants have been able to apply the same lesson more than once, in apparently different situations. It seems to happen most easily when you are naturally a quick study, committed to learning, generalizing from, and internalizing each lesson.

You have to be analytical

Consulting is NOT listening to the client and feeding him what he wants to hear. This should be obvious, but it's an all-too-common description of what many consultants do. You've probably heard the bad joke about the definition of a consultant: someone who borrows your watch to tell you what time it is.

It's important that good consultants listen well, process what they see and hear, and add value to whatever they learn. Call it independent thinking, if you prefer. It's certainly more than rephrasing what the client tells you.

Sycophants, or "yes-men," typically don't make very good consultants. They generally reinforce someone else's point of view, agree with the way things have always been done, and support others' plans and decisions. People who listen well and critically evaluate what they learn are almost always more effective as consultants. After all, it's the applied, relevant experience and creativity of consultants that make them valuable, and that means you need to be on the lookout for new ways of doing things.

Depending on the exact nature of the consulting you do, it might be important that your analytical skills include a heavy dose of quantitative assessment – perhaps statistics or financial savvy – and a better-than-average grasp of economics, arithmetic, algebra, and "understanding the numbers." That's certainly true for people in marketing, finance, R&D, engineering, and manufacturing operations -- and, in some industries, sales and general management.

While everyone on my mini-panel agreed with the importance of this aspect of consulting, three of the people with whom I spoke included it with the point below – being insightful and/or intuitive. They're clearly related, for most of us.

You have to be insightful and/or intuitive

I'm tempted to say this is the most important element on the list, but that wouldn't be completely fair. They're all important, and it would be a mistake to single out one element as being somehow more significant on the list of personal characteristics that make for successful consultants. Nonetheless, everyone with whom I spoke noted that insight (and/or intuition) is absolutely central to being a good consultant.

Also, as noted in the previous section, some associate these traits, in their own thinking, with being analytical. What they mean, I suspect, is that somehow – whether through analysis, insight, or intuition – the consultant is expected to come up with a novel solution to the client's problem. And it's the word "novel" that is operative in this case. Management consulting is a creative profession. If the client simply wanted a compilation of historical documents, for example, he'd probably have hired a research librarian on an hourly basis.

The consultant is expected to understand the situation, "read" the client team accurately, draw on prior experience, analyze and draw parallels, and come up with a solution to the problem that wasn't there before. (In some cases, the solution *might* have been there before, but wasn't recognized as the best solution until the consultant brought his or her unique perspective to bear on the issues, or recognized an interesting and instructive parallel to the client's situation from another company or industry.)

The consultant's unique contribution – and creativity – is what defines "consulting," as we're using the term. HOW the consultant comes up with the novel solution is not the client's concern. And whether analysis is a prerequisite for insight is a subject better left to behavioral psychologists and students of the creative process.

I would say that if you don't think of yourself as being creative, insightful, or intuitive, you will probably find consulting a difficult way to make a living.

You have to be a good communicator

This is another point on which everyone agreed. All the consultants felt that effective communication skills are mandatory in order to be successful as a consultant.

"Even if you are the most creative thinker, and come up with the greatest solutions for a client's problem," one of them said, "it's of no use if the client doesn't understand your recommendation, or if you present it in a way that's so confusing they don't believe it can work."

That's clearly part, but not all, of being a good communicator. The communication process is important throughout the relationship, from careful listening at the outset to effective presentation of the deliverable. If you don't listen well and understand the client's needs up-front, it's not likely you'll be able to explain persuasively what you want to do in the initial proposal, and without a sound proposal you're unlikely to get the project. If you get the project, you'll probably have to deliver progress reports that are useful to the client, or you will risk losing client confidence. And, of course, the presentation package for your deliverable is part of the deliverable itself. Communication is key from the beginning to the end of a project, and at every stage of a strong client relationship.

The need to be a good communicator includes written and oral communication, to individuals and groups, formal and informal. And it includes incoming as well as outgoing communication – part of the "good listening skills" discussed earlier as part of the "quick study" point.

I would also note, as did two of my colleagues, that really good consultants are also wonderful storytellers. They see similarities between a client's situation and one they've seen before – perhaps in a different industry – and they "tell a story" about how another manager addressed a similar problem. They include not just the bare facts but some of the emotions and secondary effects as well. They make their contribution to client education in a way that's vivid, relevant, and – yes – interesting for the audience. Consultants are not entertainers per se, but very often they can make their points more effectively with an appropriate case study, or "story," than they can with a spreadsheet full of numbers and equations.

You have to have confidence in your own abilities

Self-confidence is one of the elements we each explained a little differently, though we all agreed it was a critical requirement.

When you are retained as a consultant – an expert in your field – the clients expect you to take charge of the project and tell them what needs to be done. You are the CEO of your project, and if you don't have the confidence to assume that leadership role, your credibility will be called into question before you have a chance to do much of anything.

Without that self-confidence you'll probably feel somewhat vulnerable and project an uncertain persona to your clients. It will appear that you are seeking approval, not delivering a product that only you can deliver.

Consulting, like all creative undertakings, entails considerable personal risk, and the risk of rejection is something most of us are not eager to accept. We want our ideas to be embraced, and we want to be fully appreciated by those who count in our lives. It's easy to see why putting yourself on the line as the expert can pose a threat to your personal security.

I would point out that the successful consultants I know are all true experts and honestly believe they are the best at what they do. They project strong leadership "vibes" and give their clients a level of confidence in them that is often missing – or even absent – in new consultants, or in those who are unsure of themselves or are uncertain if consulting is right for them. They have a way of taking charge of a situation and leading their clients to the "promised land."

A great example of this was suggested by one of the consultants I interviewed. He said, "As the outside consultant-expert, you have to realize and accept that all meetings are YOURS, regardless of who calls them or what the agenda says. The client is paying you to take charge of the project, and whenever the project is being discussed in your presence, it's your meeting."

As I reflected on that comment, I smiled knowingly and re-membered many meetings in my career for which I would show up at the appointed hour in the client's conference room, not really knowing what the meeting was supposed to cover, only to have everyone looking at ME to tell them why we were gathered! It took a while for me to understand what was happening, but I finally learned that when the client invites me to a meeting he's really saying: "You're the expert. Tell us what's going on."

If I didn't have confidence in my own abilities – to lead a meeting, to understand the politics and group dynamics, to assess the status of the project, and to communicate my thoughts and advice, I'd have been dead in the water at just about every one of those meetings. Fortunately, I inherited the self-confidence gene from my parents, and I managed to survive those trials-by-fire.

Dialogue's Mission Statement

I suspect you've already noticed that these seven personal characteristics required to be a successful consultant are mostly things that you either have or you don't. It's not like you can go out and simply learn the ones that aren't innate. You certainly can improve upon each of them to some extent, but it would be a really uphill battle to try to change some deep-seated behavior patterns just because you think consulting might be interesting or attractive for you.

For example, if you don't enjoy selling, you could take some courses or read a few books on the subject. You could place yourself in situations where selling is the key function and push yourself to "try harder," but it's probably going to take a long time before you really enjoy selling. It's not impossible, just challenging.

The same is true for working alone or having high self-confidence. It's possible to learn each of those, but it's a lot easier if they come naturally to you and are part of your existing make-up. (You could learn nuclear physics, too, if it were really important to you, but most of us wouldn't make the effort if we weren't already interested in science and math.)

A lot of this became clearer to me after I'd been consulting for eight or nine years and someone asked me why I thought I'd been successful as a consultant. She was thinking of going into consulting herself, and she was looking for a mentor, I suspect. I wanted to give her a seriously-considered response, because I didn't want to be blamed if her decision didn't work out later as a result of my skewed remarks or some key consideration I failed to include. I'm keenly aware of both the attractions and drawbacks to being a consultant.

What I did is go back to a document I'd prepared earlier that presented the Mission Statement I'd crafted for my consulting firm. At one time I had given that document a lot of thought, and I figured it might be instructive for both of us if I pulled it out of the file and looked at it with fresh eyes.

Let me interject here that when you have to pull your Mission Statement out of a file to see what it says you are not using it effectively – almost by definition. To benefit most from a Mission Statement it should be posted where you can see it every day, to serve as a reminder of why you're doing what you're doing and to influence your behavior at just about every turn. Since that incident when I pulled it out of the file to see if it could help me advise my friend, I've realized this fact and made the Dialogue Marketing Group Mission Statement part of my office décor. I've reproduced it at the top of the next page.

The words in the Mission Statement, and the thoughts they express, haven't changed in the 20+ years since they were written, and they've been a clear presence – physically and emotionally – for more than half that time (after I realized how important it is to have the constant reminder on display).

If you'll compare them to the seven personal characteristics that I submit are critical to success in consulting, you'll see that they are essentially a benefit-oriented expression of virtually all of

---

Dialogue Marketing Group, Inc.

Mission Statement

Dialogue's Mission is to excite client companies with strategies and plans that will enable them to meet or exceed their objectives.

To accomplish this Mission will require that we:

√ listen well, in order to understand the goals, values and capabilities of our clients;

√ critically analyze what we learn in order to put things in proper perspective and thus guide our own independent thinking;

√ creatively apply our knowledge, skills and experience to develop strategically sound and workable plans that can, and will, meet the clients' real needs;

√ clearly and convincingly communicate our thinking, conviction and enthusiasm; and

√ support client efforts to adopt and implement agreed strategies and plans in pursuit of their own Mission and Vision.

---

them. In fact, I've had clients notice the Mission Statement plaque hanging on my wall, read it, and comment that those are the things they most want from an outside consultant. Many of them had never really thought about their expectations quite so clearly, and they found it helpful as a kind of standard or benchmark for assessing the consulting relationship.

Three of the items on our "required personal characteristics" list are between-the-lines in the Mission Statement, not explicit:

- You have to understand and love selling
- You have to like working alone
- You have to have confidence in your own abilities

That doesn't make them less important. It's only that these three, unlike the other four, do not suggest direct benefits for a client, and the Mission Statement needs to focus on the benefits a client is likely to value and appreciate.

In fact, the first one – you have to understand and love selling – is embedded in the opening phrase of the Mission Statement: "… excite client companies …" The essence of selling is to get people to care – to excite them – about the benefits your product or service will provide. Dialogue's Mission Statement could have said that we deliver strategies and plans that work, but that wouldn't capture the "selling" idea the same way "excite" does.

The other two implicit items – working alone and having confidence in your own abilities – are really expressions of our commitment to live up to the Mission Statement in total. In a sense, we're saying, "If we don't do what our Mission Statement promises, you should fire us and find someone who will." It lays the responsibility squarely on our shoulders – my own shoulders when I'm working on the project alone – and accepts full accountability for client satisfaction. That's about as much self-confidence as you can have.

We also begin to get at this in the Mission Statement when we refer to "our own independent thinking." We want to make sure clients understand that we are not going to simply repackage what they gave us and hand it back to them.

The other four characteristics are explicitly referenced in the Mission Statement:

- You have to be a quick study/student/learner
- You have to be analytical
- You have to be insightful and/or intuitive
- You have to be a good communicator

Notice, too, that the orientation of the Mission Statement is toward the client. It's as if the statement were written to be read by clients – only it wasn't. The reason for this is that I believe very strongly that a good consultant always keeps his client's best interests front-and-center in his mind, and that exceeding client expectations is what makes for successful consulting. Each time I read the Mission Statement, even casually, I am reminded that our success as consultants traces directly to the Mission Statement and to the satisfaction – the "excitement" – we are able to deliver for our clients.

Insight, creativity and intuition

This is probably the right place to deal with the issue of creativity as the central and essential characteristic of a consultant's deliverable, and to share my own perspective on the relationship between insight, intuition, and creativity.

Creativity, in this context, is defined as "novel associations that are useful." That's not my definition, but the one Roger Firestien uses. He's a recognized expert on the subject of creativity and the author of "Leading on the Creative Edge" and "Why Didn't I Think of That?" among other books, tapes, teaching materials, and programs. When I first became interested in the subject of creativity in business, I attended a seminar at which Roger was a speaker, and I have carried his definition with me ever since.

In my own mind, I have trouble separating creativity from insight or intuition. All three of them involve an ill-defined internal process that draws on knowledge or information we can't quite pinpoint, and that are characterized by output that wasn't obviously present before the process took place. Further, all three typically involve relationships between facts or ideas that were not integrally related before we "got creative" or were blessed with a new insight.

Moreover, if you examine the creative process (or insight or intuition) you'll see that it seems to be stimulated by the accumulation of information (as in learning, studying, absorbing), analysis and critical assessment, and communication or verbalization. All of these are on the list of what an effective consultant must be able to do.

In the end, of course, what counts is solving the client's problem in a way that the client probably couldn't or wouldn't have solved it himself. Remember it's the *novelty* of the solution and its *usefulness* (in solving the problem) that, by definition, make it creative.

I'm also sensitive to the fact that this whole area of creativity (or intuition, or insight) is a little uncomfortable for many professional businesspeople. For the most part they've been trained in a left-brain world that values and rewards rigorous, linear, analytical processes, and tends to evaluate ideas on the basis of what's been done before, how logical it seems, and how the numbers add up.

Creativity, by way of contrast, is almost exclusively a right-brain process, isn't subject to a formulaic, or step-by-step linear approach, and involves somewhat irrational internal "magic."

I have no need to "poke sticks at the monkeys" on this subject, so to speak, but I want to be clear that (a) I know not everyone is comfortable admitting that "creativity" is what's needed to solve a tough business problem, and (b) creativity is precisely what a client should expect from a consultant who is brought in to deliver a solution or strategy that can help a company address a particularly thorny issue.

How the consultant does it isn't the client's problem. But, if you are thinking of *becoming* a consultant, you'd be doing yourself a great disservice if you discounted the importance of this thing we're calling "creativity." And if you don't see yourself as creative (or insightful, or intuitive) you may want to reconsider your career decision.

Interpersonal skills

While we're inserting relevant and important issues, it's probably worth mentioning the so-called "people" skills as valuable assets for any consultant. There are probably some kinds of consulting where these skills are less important than others, but I can't imagine that any consultant will get very far if he isn't able to relate on a personal level to co-workers and clients. After all, clients ARE people, and they generally work in an environment with other people around them.

I'm not talking about glad-handing or faking a smile. I'm talking about treating everyone with respect, accepting people for who they are, giving them your full attention when they're talking, giving their points-of-view fair consideration, and responding in a way that demonstrates you understand them. If you feel you're somehow better than the people with whom you're working, you're bound to communicate that attitude, and it's going to be a problem for your consulting practice sooner or later.

I'm trying hard not to be "preachy" on this subject, because I would hope the importance of this skill is so obvious that this section will seem superfluous. Nonetheless, it is so critically important for most consultants that I want to be sure it IS addressed head-on and that you take the time to ask yourself if your work history indicates that people skills are among your personal assets.

Another aspect of the people consideration is your willingness to learn from everyone. Many of my most valuable lessons were taught by clients. I try very hard to listen carefully to everything they tell me, because I don't know when I'll hear similar words and thoughts again, and, more than once, I have been given high marks for being able to grasp a situation quickly simply because I felt a tinge of *deja vu*. Not only do I learn from every client, but every client is also part of my research for future consulting cases.

If there is any doubt about people skills in your own mind, consulting will probably put you to the ultimate test. You'll be dealing with people all the time, and they'll have the power to make or break you in consulting as in no other profession or career.

Business and lifestyle issues

If this book were aimed strictly at newly-minted MBAs who were considering one of the large consulting firms as a potential employer, this section probably wouldn't be here. After all, they would be employees whose jobs involve many of the elements of consulting, but they really wouldn't be self-contained consultants themselves – at least not for several years.

Because the target audience for this book includes experienced executives who are considering consulting as a between-jobs activity or second career, however, I think I'm probably obliged to include some remarks about the BUSINESS of running a one-person (or few-person) consulting firm and the LIFESTYLE implications of the decision they're about to make.

You may have noticed that the majority of this book is devoted to the actual WORK of consulting, not the business management aspect or the impact consulting is likely to have on your personal life – both of which are particularly important considerations if you're thinking of working alone or in a small group.

The business of consulting

Let's start with the business itself. A one-person consulting business is easy to start-up, can turn into a great way to make a lot of money, and requires minimal capital investment. You can even work out of your home, if you find that appealing and if you're able to cope with the administrative and home-office details. That's the good part.

The not-so-good part is that there are no assets or true equity, so you probably won't be able to convince an outside investor to fund your start-up, and you can't ever really sell your company for enough money to make a difference. There's also no leverage; all you can sell is all of your time. (The factory is idle when you're asleep – like a barber or a dentist, for example.) And customer loyalty isn't worth much, because the reason you're there is that the client's problem is a short-term one; once you've solved it the project is usually over and you need to find another source of income.

We've already covered the fact that you'll need to spend a lot of time and energy on marketing and sales, and most of that will be in advance of a formal assignment (or "on spec," as they say) – prospecting for opportunities, doing a lot of research, and presenting your credentials to managers who may not always agree with your assessment of their needs.

Conventional wisdom for a new "lone-wolf" consultant is that you should have at least a year's living expenses socked away before you start your solo business. That's how long it may take to generate enough business and collect enough consulting revenue to meet your basic needs. It would be a shame to invest, say, ten months laying the foundation for a business, and then having to give it all up because you ran out of money just two or three months before your investment paid off.

There's an interesting dilemma that awaits you, too, if you're successful at landing several clients right away. You don't want to turn business away if you can help it, of course, but what will you do if you get more business than you can handle – especially if you want to give every client 110% of your best efforts? You'll either have to hire additional qualified consultants (if you can find and afford them) or you'll have to partner with someone who can help you manage the business and the clients. Either way, you're not likely to make full margin on the "overflow" business – if you can figure out a way to handle it.

I've been through this dilemma myself, but I was fortunate to find a fully-qualified and experienced consultant, with a background similar to my own, who became my partner at a time when I'd have had to turn away business if he hadn't shown up on the right day. We work well together, have complimentary preferences and skills, and share a common philosophy when it comes to both marketing strategy and the fundamental work of consulting. We've worked together when the workload required more than one consultant, and we've worked independently when that seemed to make most sense. It's worked out well, and we've become very close friends over the years.

I'm not going to dwell in any real detail on the office management issues that face entrepreneurs with small and/or home offices. There are plenty of books that do that very well, and lots of companies and magazines that cater to new at-home entrepreneurs. You'll want to give this some thought yourself, of course, but you won't need to deal with those issues unless and until you've made the decision to consult – the real subject of this book. If you never get to that stage, there's no need to ask anyone how much copiers cost, how many phone lines you'll need, who you call for insurance, bookkeeping, tax preparation, or legal advice, how you collect past-due accounts and manage your own cash flow, or any number of other office-manager details. And you'll never need to sit down and create a pro forma monthly profit-and-loss statement or cash flow projection for your business.

Is Consulting Right For You?

On one hand, these are all important considerations that you'll probably want to address. On the other hand, don't let the tail wag the dog. First you need to decide if you want to be a consultant. Then, if the answer is yes, you will need to get into some detailed business and administrative planning.

While we're dealing with the business of consulting, it's probably worth a quick sidebar to consider another approach that comes up periodically – forming a confederation of consultants who share office space and general expenses, and refer business to one another whenever possible.

I know several consultants who have been invited to participate in arrangements like this, and I've never seen one work out well. The shared office and services are not the problems, of course; there are lots of office suites around, thanks to creative real estate agents and landlords.

The problem is thinking that somehow there's going to be a synergistic business effect from having four or five independent consultants sitting in close proximity to one another.

First of all, if a consultant is really working, he is out of the office a lot more than he is in. And when he is in, he's on the phone, crashing to get a proposal out, or a report written, or a project completed. He's busy in clients' offices, doing research, interviewing experts, networking, and looking for the next project. Having a common office and some shared services are not really of much value in terms of getting the work done.

Second, there's a good chance that the consultants who suggest this arrangement are hoping the affiliation will help THEM get new clients. They're looking at you as a source of new business for their practices, not really expecting that they will bring in new business for YOU. (Most consultants – especially new consultants – don't enjoy prospecting for new business as much as they do delivering projects or doing whatever it is they think consultants do.)

In fact, most consultants are actually reluctant to share clients – and probably for good reason. They've invested a lot of their own time and energy developing client relationships; they've gotten to know a lot about a client's problems, business philosophy, and culture; they've developed personal rapport with individuals at the client company; and they've convinced the client that they're uniquely well suited to take on a project. They've instilled confidence in themselves and their abilities, and they probably don't trust anyone else to serve the client as well as they can.

No consultant wants to risk damage to his own reputation should things not work out, and nobody wants to sacrifice or compromise hard-won client relationships by introducing a stranger – even if that "stranger" is helping to offset some of their (usually minor) overhead expenses or paying a small referral or "finder's" fee.

Finally, everyone is judged, at least in part, by the company he keeps. The individuals in a group run the risk of being tarnished by the weakest link. Nobody wants to hire a consultant who is seen as being affiliated with a loser. Somehow your affiliation with the group says something about your own standards. Even if you like everyone in the group on a personal level, you run the risk that a potential client may have a different view, and you'll be judged accordingly.

In short, please don't confuse sharing office space with good business strategy for your consulting practice. It may help cut down on expenses a bit, but it probably won't do much for building your business or enhancing your professional reputation, and it could – in some circumstances – end up hurting. It's just not worth the risk.

The consulting lifestyle

When you're out of work, almost any job looks better than what you have. I can understand why people look at consulting as a between-jobs strategy or a second career. (We'll deal with that in greater detail in Chapter 9.) Not only is it easy to get into the business, but the lifestyle looks attractive too.

Many consultants report that they like the idea of being able to adjust their schedules to allow for greater family involvement, community activities, or personal interests. They also like the idea of being able to work at home in casual dress, break for lunch when they get hungry, and set a schedule that caters to their individual sleep habits and preferences.

Some cite the variety of the work as a draw to consulting, with different clients and different problems all coexisting on their desktop simultaneously. And they love being on a first-name basis with client executives who count on them for solid, new thinking to move their businesses ahead.

There are some really nice benefits to the consulting lifestyle. But there are some drawbacks too.

Most consultants find that the stress and time pressures are far greater than they anticipated. They don't have as much time for family, hobbies, or community activities as they wanted. They're traveling more than they expected, so they're not "working at home" most of the time. And they can't relax enough to enjoy a nice lunch very often.

I also know a few people who stopped taking vacations when they began consulting. At first they didn't think they could afford a vacation, not just because it costs a lot of money but because they wouldn't be earning while they were gone, and they wouldn't be around to answer the phone if a client or potential client called. Then, when they matured and had enough business to be able to afford a vacation, they didn't feel they could, in good conscience, leave the business for long enough to get any benefit from the planned R&R. I know several folks who have gone five years without so much as a long weekend break. What kind of lifestyle is that?

Consulting is filled with peaks and valleys – highs and lows – almost all the time. It's exhilarating when you land a big project, terrifying when you realize how much work is involved and how much the client is counting on you to deliver, exciting when you get a big check in the mail, depressing when you're in the third hotel room of the week and won't be home for another four days, and really strange when you get home and hardly know what to say to your family (whom you haven't seen all week).

If that kind of seesaw life sounds enticing to you, then you may be right for consulting – at least on a personal level.

*   *   *   *   *

As I said earlier, a lot of this stuff isn't really about consulting *per se*. In fact it's more about starting your own small service business, so in a sense it's not "on topic" for this book. I include it for a couple of reasons: First, it's such an important consideration that I think I'd be remiss to dismiss or ignore it altogether. Second, when I asked consultants I know for their thoughts on what to include in this book, ALL of them included these kinds of issues – especially for people who are thinking of consulting as part of their job-search strategy or as a potentially rewarding second career.

Chapter 5

A Typical Consulting Project

As you're considering whether consulting is right for you or not, it might be useful to think about the life-cycle of a consulting project or client relationship. If you do eventually become a consultant, you'll probably get so used to this progression that you won't give it a second thought. While you're still at the beginning of the decision-making process, though, this will give you another way to project yourself into the role of consultant and see if it feels comfortable for you.

Virtually every project has nine steps or stages. Different consultants use different words to describe them, and some simplify the recipe and consolidate steps. Nonetheless, all nine elements are present in every project. As you read them and think about how they are likely to impact your life as a consultant, you'll probably find that some are very comfortable for you, while others are less so. You'll have to adapt some of the specifics to your own situation, but don't dismiss any of them too quickly, because you'll undoubtedly have to deal with them all.

The nine stages are:

1. Identifying and researching the prospective client
2. Developing the proposal, setting appropriate expectations
3. In-depth research – start-up meeting, situation analysis
4. Structuring the solution/approach
5. Analyzing data … seeking useful insights
6. Creating/defining the solution set
7. Making a recommendation and presenting the rationale
8. Developing a path-forward recommendation
9. Presenting/delivering the project in a neat, easy to approve package

In discussing these nine stages, I'm going to draw on my own experience with marketing and strategic planning issues, because those are the areas I know best and in which I have specific examples to support the points I'm going to make. I am quite certain there are parallel processes in virtually all other kinds of consulting, with the only true variables being relative importance and, of course, the actual content/subject matter addressed in the projects.

Identifying and researching the prospective client

This first stage in a consulting project can range anywhere from calling an old friend and asking if he or she has some work you can do as an outside consultant, at one extreme, to actually initiating a project and creating a preliminary situation analysis for the client on spec, at the other extreme. ("On spec" simply means that you don't actually have an assignment and that nobody has committed to paying you for the up-front work you're doing. It's something you are doing in hopes that it will lead to an assignment.)

A Typical Consulting Project

I don't have a lot of experience with the "calling-an-old-friend" end of that spectrum, but I have found that the best way to create a situation that's likely to generate new consulting projects is over-delivering on client expectations for a current project. When clients are enthusiastically positive about your work on a project, they usually do one of two things: (1) They look for additional projects they can give you (so they look even smarter for finding and retaining the outside expertise you represent); and/or (2) They tell their friends and associates how great it was working with you, effectively pre-selling you to this expanded group of potential new clients.

On my first assignment with a large business-to-business manu-facturer (a Fortune Top-25 corporation), I got really lucky and solved a huge problem for them in a way that ultimately was worth tens of millions of dollars to their bottom line. (Not a bad way to start, eh?)

That single consulting assignment – with a very modest commitment and a modest fee initially – led directly to (a) a thirteen-year relationship with that client through a series of retainers and additional projects, and (b) referrals to other departments, divisions, and business units within the company that spanned more than a decade, involved at least twenty different product categories, and generated millions of dollars in consulting fees.

It would be a great story if it ended there, but there's more. One of the senior executives with whom we worked left the company (twelve years after our initial project with him) and went to another large company. He remembered how well we'd handled a particular issue for him at the first company and called us in to address a similar project for his new company. Our work on that spawned at least half-a-dozen additional projects at company number two.

And it continued to snowball. Two different executives at company number two, and the executive from company number one, then moved to other companies, and all three of them called on us to submit proposals and take on projects for them at their new companies.

That one project that only took a few months became the rainmaker for the majority of consulting fees generated over a period of twenty years. The keys were being in the right place at the right time (i.e., having the insight to identify the client's most important problem), solving it in a creative and effective mannor, making sure we accurately and persuasively communicated our promise and positioning, and exceeding client expectations.

The other end of the spectrum ("situation-analysis-on-spec") is one we also got to know pretty well. It involves doing so much homework up front that the client can't help but be impressed with your grasp of the issues and your ability to identify creative solutions to the problem. This approach involves a lot of hard work with no guarantee of immediate success, but it's the one most of us need to use when we're first getting into consulting.

When you first hang out your shingle as a consultant, you usually sit by the phone hoping it will ring with an eager client-to-be on the other end. After a few days or weeks, it becomes clear that even calling all your friends and business contacts and announcing your availability won't deliver the project you need to get your business off the ground. So you get creative.

You identify a company that you believe has a need you can satisfy. You may do some shopping for the company's products or services, visit their website, talk to customers, assess their competition's strengths and weaknesses, read their most recent annual report and 10-K filing (or equivalent, if outside the US), see if you can find a networking contact who has additional information about the company, etc. You essentially become a one-person research department, focused on that company and the need you've identified. And your research can easily expand to cover a period of several weeks or months.

When you think you've exhausted all the sources of information, you prepare a presentation, do whatever it takes to get yourself invited to a meeting with the potential client, and present your work hoping you can persuade them that (a) you've identified a problem that's so important they can't ignore it, and (b) you're the perfect person to tackle the problem for them.

If you've done your homework well and don't offend anyone at the meeting (i.e., take full advantage of your people skills), you'll get the assignment. Otherwise, you just have to chalk it up to experience and move on to the next prospect, regardless of your personal investment to that point. Whatever you learned preparing for the meeting is yours, and it could come in handy down the road.

(I've heard a few horror stories about how a company took the work a consultant did on spec and ran with it, cutting the consultant out without so much as a "thank you," but those stories are clearly in the minority, and those companies probably are not the ones you'd have wanted to work with anyway, if you're an ethical and honorable consultant.)

At this tough end of the continuum, it's conceivable that the amount of work you do on spec would approach 20-25% of the total project, if and when you land it. I guess that's offset by the "easy" end of the continuum, though the average is probably at least 10-15% of the total – at least in my experience.

Developing the proposal, setting appropriate expectations

Once you've done the homework and presented yourself to the decision-maker, you'll need to agree on exactly what the project is. What are the objectives? What are the constraints? How soon do they need results? How much help will the client provide? Et cetera.

This is the stage, in my opinion, at which the success of the project is usually determined. Remember, your objective as the consultant is to EXCEED client expectations for the project. That means you have to establish expectations you're sure you can beat, and that the promised deliverables are attractive enough to land the project. It's a real balancing act. You want to promise great work so the client will hire you. At the same time, you want your promise to be easy enough to deliver that you're sure you can go beyond it.

Sometimes the client is so desperate for your help that the balancing act is a cakewalk. More often you need to think it through, plan your approach, and craft your proposal with the end in mind.

I remember a project that was mine for the asking. The client called, described what he needed, asked for a price and delivery date, and accepted my verbal proposal all within twenty-four hours. When I went to put it in writing, though, I began to realize how many questions I hadn't asked, how many assumptions I'd made, and how much more information I'd need that could influence the project proposal (and the timing and the fee).

Fortunately, my client appreciated my care in developing the proposal and we were able to avoid the train wreck that might otherwise have occurred. I know, however, that the opposite outcome has plagued other, less-experienced consultants more than once. Eager to close the deal, they commit too quickly. And they realize later that the client was expecting far more than they were willing or able to deliver. That is usually the end of the consultant's relationship with that client.

In the next chapter we'll deal with the proposal itself, pricing your services, and how you can showcase all your up-front homework for maximum advantage. For now, the real point of the discussion is that the care you put into developing the proposal will directly affect client expectations and your ability to exceed them.

A Typical Consulting Project

In-depth research –
start-up meeting, situation analysis

No matter how much up-front work you've done or how much the client has briefed you on the project, once it's approved you'll want to have a formal start-up meeting so that all the client players can have a chance to share their perspectives, biases, and unique needs "on the record."

Actually, the start-up meeting is arguably the second most important determinant of a consultant's success. It's another chance to be sure everyone understands the deliverables (i.e., to establish appropriate expectations that you will plan to exceed). It also provides the consultant with a broad perspective on the issues and the sensitivities of people who are in the trenches and intimately familiar with the company, culture, industry, competition, and other elements that can directly affect the project's outcome.

If the client ever suggests skipping the formal start-up meeting, the alarms should go off in your head and the red flags should begin flying. The project will almost certainly be doomed if you don't find a way to have that meeting.

The start-up meeting is the beginning (or a critical point, if you've already done some advance work) of the situation analysis. And the reason you want to complete a formal situation analysis is two-fold: First, you want to gather as much relevant information as you can for later analysis (and as fodder for your insights); second, you want to be sure you understand the facts properly and identify any discrepancies between what you learn and what the client believes to be the case.

If you and the client can't agree on the situation analysis, the chances they'll buy your solution and recommendation are slim. On the other hand, if you and the client are in lockstep agreement on the operating environment and situation, then you've gone a

71

long way toward pre-selling your solution as the best, most appropriate one – even before you know what it is.

I always try to leave the start-up meeting not only with complete notes on the client's perceptions of the problem and view of the situation, but also with as much reading material as possible. I ask the client for any internal documents that bear on the subject, suggested trade journals or magazine articles that might give me a better perspective on the industry, and a preliminary list of the 10 or 12 people with whom I might speak for additional background and input. The list might include company employees or managers in other functional areas, front-line sales representatives or brokers, customers, and/or strategic partners and suppliers.

Structuring the solution/approach

Once you have an initial crack at the situation analysis, it's probably a good idea to figure out how you're going to use what you've learned in addressing the client's key question(s).

I've found that very often the initial situation analysis raises new questions, which then have to be researched before you can actually address the issues head-on. You can uncover these by asking yourself how you would approach a structured solution to the client's problem based on what you know, and what other information might be helpful.

When I had a project in agricultural chemicals, for example, I spent several months working on farms and interviewing farmers in Nebraska, Iowa, Illinois, and Indiana. I actually learned a lot about agriculture, the farm lifestyle, and the business aspects of farming. I also learned that successful farmers had another side to their lives that none of us – the clients or the consultants – had anticipated: the management of financial risk.

A Typical Consulting Project

Local banks typically finance virtually all of a farmer's up-front expenses, and every feed store has a real-time display of commodity futures prices from the major exchanges. There is a "shadow world" of risk management going on right beside the actual crop-growing aspect of farming. I'm not sure why that came as such a surprise, except that nobody had ever mentioned it at the start-up meeting, nor was it referenced in any of the documents the client provided for our education on their product or target market. And, since I grew up in the city, all of this farming stuff was new to me.

What this new awareness triggered was another round of field interviews, this time with the bank lending officers and commodity futures brokers in farm communities. Only when we had that piece of the puzzle in hand were we really prepared to analyze what we'd learned and develop an approach to solving the client's problem.

The challenge in this phase of the project is to be sure you're fully informed about all the issues that impact the situation. It's where an outside perspective can add real value to the client's perceptions of the marketplace, and it's often central to a novel and effective solution that will make the consultant a real hero.

In the case of the project in agricultural chemicals, we recommended promotion and communication to a critical additional target audience – the bankers who had a major financial stake in minimizing the risk of crop damage. The client bought our approach and changed the way they promoted the product the following season. The result was dramatically expanded market penetration and record sales for the client's brand.

Analyzing data ... seeking useful insights

When you're pretty sure you have all the information, it's time to immerse yourself in it, analyze it, identify relationships that others may have missed, and track down the source of any anomalies or discrepancies in what you've read, heard, or seen.

There are two reasons to be especially careful and diligent in this phase: First, you'll want to present your findings and analysis to the client as part of the rationale for your conclusions and recommendations. If you've been careful during the analysis phase, it will be a snap to present your work, and you won't have to go through it twice – once for "go" and a second time for "show."

The second reason is that your creative brain gets its best insights when it has lots of information, thoughts, memories, images, and analyses available as stimulation. It's a necessary part of the creative process for most of us, and since we live by our creative output, the analysis of information is really the raw material of which our deliverable is made.

Many times – perhaps as often as half the time – the insights we get require that we reframe the original question. Perhaps the original question was sub-optimal or had implications other than the ones the client intended. That's OK. It's as much of a contribution to ask the right question as to answer it creatively. Many times we've taken on a project and gone to the client midstream to suggest a modification of the project objective, or a new slant on the original objective.

In almost every case, the client's reaction is surprise and gratitude for our creative interpretation of the situation. They see our reframing of the issue as adding real value with a fresh perspective. They appreciate our creative input and our willingness to think outside the box.

There's a great temptation to try to combine the first few phases of a project – particularly when the client is pushing for answers fast. They ask why we can't be thinking creatively while we're still compiling the situation analysis, or why we want a separate, time-consuming phase of the project before we develop our recommendations.

It's usually a very sorry consultant who responds to the client with a "good soldier" approach – "OK, I'll be a good soldier, skip those middle steps, and just give you my recommendations" – because creative problem solving requires "gestation time." New ideas don't just show up on demand, and they seem to avoid showing up at all when you feel there's a gun to your head or a clock ticking somewhere in the background. You certainly don't feel you can take the time to ask yourself if the original question was the right one.

I always tell impatient clients that a well-reasoned solution to their problem is better than a knee-jerk reaction and that, as consultants, we live by our reputation for giving clients the best advice, not by completing projects on a break-neck schedule.

I explain that we cannot get nine women to have the baby in just one month. The process takes time, and anything we do to try and compress that time runs a very real risk of compromising the quality of the result. Some things just have to run their course.

Some of the most difficult decisions we've had to make in managing our consulting business have dealt with the issue of fastest-versus-best. When the client has a real need for critical timing – like a seasonal product introduction, for example – we often ask ourselves if we're doing the client any favors by agreeing to a project we know won't be our best work in order to meet a timing requirement. We ask ourselves (and often the client) if everyone would be better served delaying a few months (or even a year) if the plan were twice as good, or if there's some first-to-market advantage that outweighs the importance of having a great project deliverable.

It's never an easy decision – especially for us. We might have to walk away from a very lucrative project because we don't want to take the risk of disappointing the client with a less-than-great solution as a result of tight timing. On the other hand, we always ask ourselves, what's likely to happen if the client tries to do this by himself, without our input, in order to make a tight deadline? Can we add enough value with a gun to our heads to justify the time, effort, and cost?

We have cases where we took the project, knowing it was a risk, and we have a few where we declined because the risk seemed more than we were willing to accept. If the project fails because the consultants did a lousy job, nobody will remember that it was completed in record time.

Creating/defining the solution set

When we think we know the right answer to the right question, we usually challenge ourselves to come up with a few viable alternatives. This isn't an exercise to invent straw-man options to make our recommendation look like the best one. It's to challenge ourselves to come up with even better alternatives than we first uncovered.

We've learned over the years that the first answer isn't always the best one. It may have elements of a great solution, but it's rare that we can't improve on a good idea. That's why we ask ourselves, "If the client doesn't like our recommended approach, what other alternatives might be more acceptable?"

If we can develop a range of viable options, then we can lay out the pros and cons of each one and select the one that's most comfortable or most likely to yield the desired result. Clients almost always prefer this approach to the "I-know-what's-best-so-listen-to-me" challenge, and I don't blame them. I am always skeptical when someone comes to me with only one option and tries to convince me "it's the only way."

It probably won't surprise you to learn that as often as not we DO come up with better solutions in this phase of the project, or we come up with questions and approaches that are different from what the client might have expected going in. We try to consider each solution from a number of perspectives, and sometimes the initial solution is likely to be preferred by one department, while an alternative would be preferred by another.

One time when this occurred we liked two alternatives quite a bit, and we couldn't decide ourselves which to recommend. Because the client relationship was a long-standing one, and we were comfortable sharing our approach-approach dilemma with them, we actually presented the client with both directions – called A and B, for simplicity – and asked them for some input and direction.

We were a little surprised at the intensity of the debate that ensued at the client's office; it lasted almost a month, with the Sales VP claiming that they couldn't execute alternative A, and the Finance VP claiming that alternative B (the one Sales preferred) could get out of control and cost more than was budgeted – especially if it was successful. We ended up having to develop a hybrid plan – a version of B that had some built-in cost controls to eliminate the risk of overspending, even though it also capped the possible immediate return and long-term profit potential.

For the record, we actually presented five alternative plans, not two. All of them were viable, and each had advantages (and disadvantages) of some kind. We recommended plans A and B as our preferred approaches, anticipating that there would be differences of opinion as to how much risk could be tolerated and how easy the plans would be to implement and control. The client agreed that A and B were preferred over the other three, but couldn't agree on which to embrace. And, for those of you who are curious, B was our initial plan, with the others developed as viable alternatives when we considered possible drawbacks and alternate approaches.

The point of all this is that developing a range of alternatives usually results not only in a better recommendation but also better client buy-in to the selected alternative. And it almost always smokes out any hidden issues that escaped scrutiny when the original statement of project objectives was developed. In the example above, no one ever specified that sticking to the budget was more important than generating incremental sales volume at payout levels, even though that turned out to be the guiding principle.

Making a recommendation and presenting the rationale

It has been my experience, and that of most other consultants with whom I've spoken, that the presentation of a project is almost as important as the substance. I'm not sure this is true for all kinds of consulting, but it's interesting that nobody has challenged this or discouraged me from making the point.

The "packaging" for your deliverable says a lot about you, and it can affect the way a client reacts to you (and to your advice). That's why we always try to share our rationale, thinking process, and any biases with the client very explicitly. And we always present our recommendations clearly, with full back-up detail in a format that's comfortable for the client.

And even when the client doesn't request a written document as part of the deliverable, we make sure to provide a leave-behind or summary of our thinking and presentation, because we know that someone someday will ask "Whose idea was that?" or "Why did they want us to do it that way?" and the documentation will save us from having to rethink the project ourselves. It also keeps our name in front of the client in a tasteful way.

I mention this because if you don't budget and plan on time for developing your presentation, you'll probably regret it. It takes time to organize your thinking, commit it to writing (or to an electronic presentation format), and to edit, adjust, and/or practice your delivery. The presentation is very much a part of the project, just like the other phases, and it will surely be included in the client's assessment of your overall performance.

Like packaging of other kinds, the presentation quality can't substitute for the content or substance of the project, but carelessness in packaging can undermine your credibility, detract from the value of the deliverable, and "poison the well" for future projects or recommendations. Don't make the mistake of thinking the client "doesn't care" about the package.

Even small things like spelling or grammar, or leaving out a support point in the explanation of your rationale, will communicate lack of thoroughness and inattention to detail. Why do that to yourself, especially if you've put in the time and effort to deliver an otherwise stellar project performance?

Two other points worth making: Generally the client is expecting a specific recommendation from the consultant. That's essentially what they've contracted for, and they have every reason to insist on it. We always challenge ourselves to be very clear and explicit about our recommendations. In fact, we usually label them clearly with something like "Recommended Approach" in bold letters, so the skeptics can't accuse us of ambiguity when it comes to declaring our point of view.

I mention this because new consultants sometimes are reluctant to put themselves on the line and commit to a position. They're afraid that they'll blow the project if the client rejects their recommendation, or they think that they'll somehow be better served to simply offer up a laundry list of alternatives without making a recommendation of their own.

Perhaps this is part of the basic requirement we discussed earlier: A consultant has to have high self-confidence, be willing to make clear decisions about what he or she thinks will be in the client's best interests, and then defend those decisions if or when challenged.

The second point deals with the bigger picture. One of the filters we always put our recommendations through is the "implications" of what we're recommending. Very often a consultant's recommendations have side effects, by-products, or ramifications within the client organization, beyond the scope originally anticipated. We think we're obligated to at least identify these for our client, so that he or she can anticipate them and allow for any additional communication that will make everything work better in the final analysis. Besides, it never hurts for the consultant to be seen as taking the big-picture view and keeping the long-term vision in mind.

This may differ based on the kind of consulting you do. In marketing and strategic planning it's certainly very important, and when there are several interdependent work groups in the client company it's just a good idea to ask yourself how your recommendation will affect each of them. Perhaps you can even identify specific benefits or by-products of the project that will make life easier for another department or individual.

Developing a path-forward recommendation

As part of the presentation of recommended actions, we always include a step-by-step path forward for the client. This is an itemized list of what the client would need to do if they are in agreement with our proposed course of action. It includes a rough timetable, assignment of responsibilities, likely cost and benefits, and some clear way to measure and track progress ("key milestones"). In short, it's a road map of the path ahead.

Occasionally it's appropriate to make this part of a subsequent meeting, perhaps a week or two after the presentation of results and recommendations. For example, when we present a project with two or three possible approaches, it may not make sense to spend a lot of time on path-forward details until a specific approach has been determined and agreed. This takes a little pressure off the client at the presentation meeting without leaving him in a quandary when it comes to the path forward.

Clients really appreciate having this step included because it makes clear what the impact of the recommendation will be on their individual to-do lists in the near-term. It lets them know how many people will be required, how much management time will be involved, and what kind of time pressures they can expect. It also gives the consultant an opportunity to offer his or her services in subsequent steps, if he can bring additional value to the project.

I would estimate that at least 30-40% of our consulting revenues have been the result of offers to continue in a consulting role during implementation of plans and proposals we initially developed, and virtually all of those offers were part of a path-forward recommendation when we delivered the project. This is not only good business for the consultant, but it also says to the client that the consultant is confident enough in his or her recommendation to stick with it through implementation.

Presenting/delivering the project in a neat, easy to approve package

While I suspect this may not be as important in some kinds of consulting as in others, we've found that often clients want to think about our recommendations for a few days before making a decision. They want to discuss things internally (i.e., without the consultant present) or they want to have someone else look at the recommendations and offer input or comments. (It could be another executive, boss, legal counsel, etc.)

In any event, we always review the whole deliverable package – the report, presentation, executive summary, everything – with an eye toward how easy it will be for someone to approve it. Ideally, it would be as simple as having them say "I agree with this and would like everyone to do his part to make it happen." In order to get to that point, we want to be sure it's crystal clear what they're being asked to agree to, and to identify the benefits, costs, and implications of the decision.

This is an excellent discipline for the consultant – regardless of the client's reaction – because it forces him to really focus on the value he brings to the project, the way it's presented to the client, and the way it's all tied together. If the proposal isn't easy for the client to approve, it's probably because the consultant hasn't thought through all the issues.

Investing in the project up-front

In some kinds of consulting, the process for thinking through the phases of a project or client relationship is quite extensive. It's called "developing a proposal" but it's much more than just creating the document. For these consultants, developing a thorough proposal is time consuming and can entail a substantial up-front investment.

I know of one company where the cost to prepare and submit a proposal is well in excess of $25,000 – sometimes a large multiple of that amount. The reason they accept this is that the average project they propose generates fees on the order of tens of millions of dollars, with profit margins large enough to offset the cost of many, many proposals that don't get accepted. It's good business for them.

For a small consulting practice, where it's essentially you, there's no way you can match the up-front investment of a company like that. It wouldn't be appropriate even if you could. The point, though, is that you don't just walk in and volunteer your services without thinking through all the aspects of the relationship and phases of the project. In fact, you'll do yourself a big favor if you take your time and give the subject your full attention before you begin your initial approach.

Chapter 6

The Consulting Proposal

I think it's probably appropriate that we devote a chapter to the subject of the consulting proposal itself. That document plays several roles: it's a selling piece, a contract, a blueprint for the project – and it's another way to look at consulting to see whether it's comfortable and right for you.

Once again I'm going to presume that you're thinking about general management or marketing consulting and present the information in a format that is specific to that genre. As before, it shouldn't take much imagination to transform the basic principles into a guideline for any kind of true consulting, and the embedded marketing principles will certainly apply to all.

Of course, there are some consulting areas in which the proposal will be much more detailed and complex. It's unlikely there are many where it will be simpler. What I'd suggest is that you consider the approach outlined here for the underlying principles. Then decide for yourself what fits your own needs, what your clients would expect, and how you can develop a proposal format that works for you.

Most of our proposals follow a fairly standard and proven format. They include the following seven sections:

1. Overview/Executive Summary
2. Background
3. Summary of Proposal
4. Work Plan
5. Staffing
6. Timing and Fees
7. Next Steps

Most proposals require 7-10 pages of single-spaced, 11-point text, plus one or two exhibits or appendices if appropriate, and we ALWAYS ensure that the wording is precise, there are no typographical errors, and that no important points have been omitted. We see the proposal as a kind of "free sample" of the work we do. We want the prospective client to say to himself, "I want a final product for this project that's as precise and thorough as the proposal."

Think for a few moments about why each section of the proposal is so important and how you can use the proposal as a tool for making your own decision to consult or not. Actually prepare a proposal for the project you'd like to land and see if it's something you'd be comfortable having as your own marching orders. Remember that old saying: "Be careful what you ask for; you might get it."

Overview/Executive Summary

The opening paragraph or two – rarely more than four or five sentences total – are for the specific purpose of grabbing the client's attention and giving him a reason to read further, keeping him from sending the entire document to the circular file posthaste. While the purpose is quite straightforward, crafting the words often takes a bit longer than you'd think at first.

The first sentence should state the specific nature of the proposal and the key benefit the client will realize as a result of having the project in hand. If it doesn't do that, the client may think the proposal should go to someone else, or that it's not worth the time it will take to read through "all that verbiage." It also should state the problem, or project definition, in terms that are familiar to the prospective client so that no interpretation or translation is required. As with most effective communication, simplicity and directness are key.

The remaining sentences may either amplify the initial sentence or add other critical information, such as when the project will start/finish, important ancillary benefits, immediate risks inherent in deferring or avoiding the project, or longer-term implications. I'd estimate that about half of our proposals begin with just an introductory paragraph of one or two sentences. We usually feel that if we can't make our point that quickly and directly we haven't thought it through enough ourselves.

Background

The background section is a little longer and begins to set the stage for why the client should assign the project to you. Its purpose is to lay out the key situational factors that make this an important project, and to demonstrate to the client that you understand their business well enough to be the right person to tackle it.

The challenge in this section is to showcase your homework well enough to give the client some confidence in your grasp of the situation without rambling on about all the "other things" you've learned. You want to make every effort to include only those facts that are directly germane to the problem you plan to address, yet cover all aspects of the background that might bear on your proposal.

Sometimes we are tempted to include graphs or tables of information that demonstrate very clearly why we've reached a certain conclusion in our situation analysis. Occasionally we do just that. More often we simply summarize the key thought and refer the client to an exhibit or appendix for detailed support. What's important is not interrupting the flow of what you're saying or forcing the client to shift gears in thinking about the point you are making.

The background section is a good place to get the client nodding in agreement with the key elements of a situation analysis so that the actual project proposal will seem like the right and logical next step. Try to keep it brief and to the point, but include all the relevant background so you can't be accused of missing anything that's really important.

Summary of Proposal

The summary of the actual proposal, with a very clear deliverable (so labeled) and explicit client benefits, comes next. This section restates or paraphrases the first sentence or two in the opening executive summary, and then expands on it as appropriate for the project.

At a minimum it should highlight or dramatize the importance of the benefits to the client, and deal openly with any obvious reservations the client might have. The purpose of this section is to give both the client and the consultant a clear understanding of what success looks like for this project. If the client is sold on the importance of achieving that success, everything else is simply reassurance that you can deliver it.

Usually this section is three or four paragraphs and it includes a very specific statement of the project objectives, key deliverables, and timing. Of course, it also makes clear the benefits the client will realize if/when the project is successfully completed (i.e., WHY he should want the project at all). The one thing it does not include is a discussion of the nuts-and-bolts of how you're going to tackle the problem or address the situation. That's in the next section.

Work Plan

The detailed work plan often comprises at least half the total proposal. It lays out exactly what you plan to do, how you plan to do it, how long each step will take, which steps are sequential and which can be concurrent, what the requirements and prerequisites are for each step, and what involvement will be required on the client's part during each phase of the project. It also includes a disclosure of who owns intellectual property generated in the course of delivering the project and any other legal or questionable issues.

If you're in a field where the project entails substantial risk for the client, you'll want to spell that out, discuss how you plan to manage and mitigate that risk, and ensure that it's clear to everyone what liability you're accepting (or not accepting). This is the consulting equivalent of malpractice insurance.

We typically start by breaking the project into phases – usually three or four of them, occasionally five – and giving an overview of the whole process. Then we discuss each phase in some detail, including any ramifications of what we plan to do. If there's ever a question about how we went about delivering the project, this section is the "official reference." It's the meat of the contract between the client and the consultant, and it also helps *us* think about what's likely to be involved in the project before we "own" it. That's key.

Experience has taught us how to describe each aspect of what we plan to do, how specific to be, how much latitude to reserve for subsequent modifications, and how much we would rely on client input/cooperation for each phase. You'll need to determine that for yourself, and it will probably be somewhat different for each kind of consulting, if not for each project.

The important point to remember is that this is the guts of your proposal; it's what you plan to *do* in order to produce the deliverables for which you're contracting.

Staffing

We usually include a section in the proposal that lets the client know who will be working on the project, which tasks, if any, will be outsourced, and why the people we plan to involve in the project are the right individuals.

If we're new to the client, we are very specific about WHY we're the right people – listing as many as five or six reasons, and supporting each important point with specific examples of relevant prior experience. We want them to be as comfortable with us, as individuals and being right for the project, as we are with them and the project requirements.

Understand that this is NOT a recitation of your resume. It's client-focused, and looks a lot like the spec sheet the client might have developed if he'd come up with the project and created the list of requirements for the ideal consultant to take on the project. In that sense, this is yet another test of your understanding of the client's mind-set and the important issues facing the client company. It's not a place to flaunt your personal accomplishments, list every detail of your prior experience, or stroke your ego.

We're usually careful here to focus on true qualifications, not on education, training courses, or other "pedigree" items. There's a real tendency to make this an ego-serving section, and that would be self-defeating. Ask yourself if each point you make is more important to the client than it is to you. If the answer is "yes," then leave it in. Otherwise, see if you can turn it around so that it becomes a client-oriented point.

For example, do you think the client really cares whether you have an MBA or not? Do you think the client even cares if you graduated from college? I suspect not. The client cares if you can deliver an end-result that will mean more money to his bottom line. That's all. Instead of dragging the client through your personal history, focus on why you are so perfect for this project.

Remember Grigori Rasputin? He was semi-literate, uneducated, and had questionable ethics and reprehensible moral values. Yet he delivered on the Tsarina's project (i.e., stopped the bleeding and saved the life of her hemophiliac son) and earned his way to a position of trusted influence on decisions that affected the entire Russian Empire. His personal background and pedigree didn't matter one iota.

Let's bring the point closer to home: I once bought a small, struggling manufacturing company. My plan was to inject some smart marketing, build up the sales and profit, and sell the company within five years for a multiple of the improved earnings. It worked, and I was really proud of what I was able to do.

Then a few years later we were trying to land a consulting project with a client in a similar industry, facing a situation similar to the one I'd faced when I bought my company. I wanted to be sure the client knew what I could do for them, and I wanted to cite my experience with the manufacturing company I'd bought, built, and sold. I didn't want to flaunt my success, though, because the circumstances weren't exactly parallel, and I wasn't really sure I could do the same thing for the prospective client. I didn't want their expectations to outstrip my own capabilities.

What we did in the staffing section of the proposal was simply say that we'd had experience with successfully enhancing marketing programs in industries similar to theirs. We cited the percent increase in sales (in my company) over a multi-year period, and indicated that the marketing programs were a large part of the reason for the growth. The fact that I had actually purchased the company, and then sold it for a nice profit, wasn't relevant. It was important to me, of course, but it really wasn't relevant to the client so we left it out. We also left out the fact that I have an engineering degree, an MBA, and some PhD-level studies. That information simply wasn't relevant.

I'm sure you get the idea. The staffing section is more than just a disclosure in the contract you're developing with the client. It's also a subtle selling section – and one that's especially valuable if you're competing with other consultants for the project.

Oh, and yes, we got the project with that manufacturing company; and we made such a remarkable contribution that the company was purchased by a larger competitor just a year after our project ended. And it was our project – the new marketing program – that first captured their attention!

Timing and Fees

While this section would seem pretty straightforward, it is actually the most difficult to get right, at least for most consultants. You want to make the terms explicit, you want them to be attractive to the client, and you want to be fair to yourself as well. Let's deal first with timing.

Timing

The timing discussion is a two-edged sword: You want to make your proposal appealing to the client (who almost always wants the project finished immediately), and you want to be sure you give yourself enough time to do things well and/or manage additional projects running simultaneously and competing for your attention. Remember, your objective as the consultant is to over-deliver against the client's expectations. If you're too aggressive in your timing estimate, how likely do you think it will be that you'll finish early?

You also want to be clear about the timing for interim deliverables and status meetings and reports. You are setting expectations in this section that you'll have to live with (and want to exceed), so it pays to consider everything carefully.

Fees

Fees are another issue, and one that warrants a much more detailed discussion. Let's start with the three philosophical approaches to establishing consulting fees:

- *Hourly or per-diem* – where you're essentially selling your time (e.g., $1,800 per day, or $225 per hour, etc.)
- *Retainer* – where you're committing a percentage of your mind and body for a defined period of time (e.g., 25% of my time for the next 6 months, etc.)
- *Project* – a flat fee for the agreed deliverables according to the work plan

Here's my assessment of those options for a new consultant:

- I would submit that the first option – *hourly or per-diem billing* – is in nobody's best interest. The consultant is motivated to be inefficient and take as long as possible to complete the task. He also has to keep detailed records of how much time is spent and how much of that should be billable. The client is motivated to minimize contact with the consultant, because the "meter is ticking" every time there's a phone call or e-mail message. Clients typically spend as little time briefing the consultant as possible, because they know that each hour they spend is costing them money. And they have to trust the consultant to accurately account for his time and bill honestly. It's the formula for a failed relationship.

- ***Retainer billing*** is much better, though it usually applies to a consulting arrangement AFTER the initial project. It's difficult to pin down a deliverable, so success is a matter of "trust-me-it's-working." I've billed in retainer mode with several clients over the years, but virtually every one of these arrangements came in the second or third year of an ongoing relationship. In one case, for example, we delivered a marketing strategy project the first year, and then offered to continue during implementation. The client anticipated that implementation would take at least a year, so they asked us for a proposal to continue in a consultative role during that year, without a specific deliverable and without a fixed number of days or hours. We agreed to "be available as required" to provide guidance and direction in the implementation of the strategic plan we'd developed. In return the client paid us an agreed amount every quarter, and we reviewed our time demands on a regular basis to be sure we each felt the agreement was fair in both directions.

Because we always want to be seen as over-delivering, we usually look for a way to go beyond the written agreement when we're in a retainer relationship, or to "carry over" a portion of the last quarter's billing into the next year – essentially giving the client an extra month, or "baker's dozen," of our services. Our objective is to have clients feel they are receiving very high value for their commitment to the arrangement.

- *Project billing*, in my opinion, is the fairest approach for both the client and the consultant. The deliverables and timing are clear, and the fee is established based on fair-market pricing – it's what the client is willing to pay and the consultant is willing to accept. What this does is two things: (1) It motivates the consultant to work as efficiently as possible (fewer hours spent means a higher average hourly rate); and (2) It ensures that the client pays for value received, not for how many hours or days the consultant has to spend to deliver the project.

In my practice, I absolutely refuse to bid on projects where the fee must be stated in per-diem terms. I've found it always ends in a disappointment for one party or the other. I accept retainers only when I'm comfortable that the relationship is strong enough that we trust each other completely, and only after we've worked on a project basis first.

There's another reason why project billing is a great way to start: it forces the consultant to think rigorously not only about what's involved and what the work plan will require, but also what the benefit should be worth to the client. If the likely result of the project will be an increase of $5 million to the client's bottom line, the project may well be worth a fee of $500,000. It doesn't matter how much time it will take or what daily rate the consultant wants. On the other hand, if the result will be only

$150,000 in bottom line benefit, the consultant's fee can't very well exceed that amount — again regardless of the time required.

A smart consultant will discipline himself to calculate the likely dollar value of a project before he finalizes the proposal, to be sure the fee is in line with both the value to the client and the consultant's own time/earnings needs. Jumping at a per-diem billing arrangement usually means the consultant is too lazy to go through this process, and — most of the time — is more focused on his own needs (for time and/or revenue) than on the client's value received.

Of course, there's more to the Timing and Fees section than the literal timing and fees. You'll want to spell out the terms and timing of payment, whether there are additional charges (travel expenses, etc.), and whether there is any provision for changes in the deliverable that might affect timing or cost on your part. These will undoubtedly vary based on the kind of consulting you do, but they should be stated explicitly up-front, so there is no basis for misunderstanding later.

We typically request a portion of the fee in advance, a portion midway through the project, and the balance on completion. Of course, if the project is a short one, and the fee is relatively small, we bill it in fewer installments — for our convenience and the client's.

We almost always make travel expenses a re-billable item, not because we couldn't simply include it in the project cost, but because we want the client to think twice before sending us on a trip that might not be necessary. If there's an additional expense as a result of extra travel, the client is less likely to send us on trips that will probably have a marginal payback.

Finally, we usually give the client some rationale for the fee in this section. If the fee is higher than the client might have expected, we explain why. We want them to understand the value they're getting, not just the cost. If it's lower than they might have expected, we want them to understand that we're not sacrificing quality, and we explain the basis for the lower fee. In short, we want the client to be comfortable that we've given this aspect of our proposal the same careful attention we'll be giving their project if we get the job and that we're striving for fairness in both directions – a win-win relationship.

Next Steps

The last section of the proposal is an invitation to the client to take the next step and approve the project – assuming that's what you want them to do. You have to make it clear how you expect them to proceed if they agree with what you've suggested. Do you want the proposal to serve as the agreement between you? If so, there needs to be a place for them to "sign on the dotted line," and it needs to be clear what happens after that. And you want to be sure the client understands that accepting your proposal is essentially the same as issuing a purchase order for your services.

We usually suggest a phone call to let us know if the proposal is accepted, followed by signed hard-copy documents (one for them, one for us) to be sure we're agreeing on the same project specs. We also remind the client that the written agreement protects us both and that we will be using the document to be sure we deliver every-thing they expect – and more. (What if the decision-maker is gone by the time the project is done? What if you are unable to finish the project for some reason? You get the idea.)

We also schedule the start-up meeting immediately upon acceptance, and say we'll do that in the "Next Steps" section of the proposal. We want the client to share our feelings of excitement and eagerness to begin, and not to think that once the project is approved we'll retreat into hiding for weeks on end.

* * * * *

As you reflect on the elements of a consulting proposal, as described above, are you comfortable that you can live by the terms of a proposal that YOU would create for a client? Take a look at the proposal I developed for a prospective client (in Appendix B) and see if it gives you any additional ideas. It's for a fairly large project, but the thinking process and presentation are just the same if the project is smaller.

And if you have any doubts, I encourage you to create a proposal for <u>your own services</u> to <u>your ideal client</u>, and see if the process makes things any clearer for you. You'll probably be surprised at how many issues crop up as you're writing, how many questions are raised "between the lines," and how many aspects of consulting you simply haven't recognized before.

Chapter 7

Consulting From the Client's Perspective

Having now reviewed consulting in some detail from the consultant's point of view, it's a good idea to look through the other end of that telescope to see what consulting looks like from the client's perspective.

Because I've been in marketing most of my professional life, it's impossible for me not to think first about the customer in considering any business decision – including the one to enter consulting as a second career. This may sound strange to some of you, because I've noticed that when people are dealing with personal issues – decisions about their future, for example – they tend to focus primarily on their own needs, values, beliefs, and behaviors. They list pros and cons, advantages and disadvantages, strengths and weaknesses, opportunities and threats – all from their own perspective. They think it's "all about them" – and, I guess, in a way it is.

But in another way it's not. Marketing is all about understanding the customer's needs. Once you do that you have a chance to determine whether or not you can satisfy those needs. And, if you can, you then have to determine how to communicate the story and the benefits to customers, how to deliver the product or service at a price and on terms that will be attractive to them, and ultimately whether you can both be winners in the transaction.

Anyone who pursues a business venture – or markets his services as a consultant – is doomed to failure if he doesn't first take this kind of marketing perspective. If there's no customer, there's no business.

So as you begin to think about yourself as a consultant, it's a good idea – perhaps even a prerequisite if you want to be successful – to take a hard look at your future customers. Clients have a lot in common with you that actually can help you assess whether consulting is up your alley.

Lack of skills or time

First, consulting clients have important needs that they are not able to meet themselves. Either they don't have the time or manpower, or they don't have the necessary skills. If they did, they probably wouldn't be hiring an outside consultant. Often the need is one that either doesn't occur very often and/or is relatively short-term (and doesn't warrant hiring a full-time, permanent employee) – like developing a positioning platform for a new product, or selecting an advertising agency, or establishing a new pricing policy, to name a few examples from my own consulting experience.

I know a consultant who works exclusively with sales professionals, giving them tools to master conceptual selling and a process that provides rapid feedback. She is typically called in when there are new salespeople who have been in technical or support positions before, and for whom the sales function is a new role. She works with them for a month or so, comes back for a review a few months later, and she's finished with the project in less than four months total.

In most companies, having someone like that on-staff wouldn't make much sense. She'd be sitting around doing nothing most of the time – just waiting for a new salesperson with a technical background to show up. As an outside consultant, she delivers high value quickly, earning her fee and solidifying her role with a client company every time. Even if the cost to hire her were the same as her consulting fee, the client company would rather not have an employee sitting around idle most of the time. It sets a terrible precedent and example for everyone else, and she'd probably learn to hate her job very quickly. (It's really boring when you have nothing to do.)

Outside perspective is critical

A second reason clients hire outside consultants is the need for an objective view of the issues and for the opportunity to learn from experience in other industries, other companies, and parallel situations. It's really difficult to see the forest when you're in the middle of all those trees, and many companies are so wrapped up in their own unique culture and industry baggage that they really can't see the bigger picture without help from the outside.

Even if they can identify the key elements of the situation analysis accurately, most individuals don't have the breadth of exposure to other industries and other companies to recognize parallel situations when they do exist.

One of the best examples of this is creating a positioning platform for a new product or service. The process for this is fairly straightforward: you learn everything you can about the product; you research the market in great detail; you look for a natural "fit" between the product benefits and the market needs; and you express that fit in a structured statement that becomes the positioning statement (or platform).

There are a number of widely accepted criteria for a good positioning statement, and you have to know what they are. It also helps to understand the implications of a positioning statement – how it impacts all the areas of the marketing mix and the business plan. You can't create a positioning platform in an intellectual vacuum. Even with the recipe and the check-list, however, positioning isn't something that most people – even experienced, professional marketers – can do easily.

The reason for this is two-fold: First, positioning isn't something you do very often. A new positioning platform is something you create *once* for a product, not every week, or month, or year. That means a typical marketing professional will only have a few opportunities to deal with original positioning in a 40-year career. There may be some minor adjustments – even a re-positioning – periodically, but even that will be every 5-10 years, not every six months or every year.

Second, the issues involved in positioning a product are much easier to anticipate and deal with when you've created dozens, or even hundreds, of positioning platforms. It's experience with the positioning process that makes it easier; the specifics of the product or the marketplace are much less important. A positioning statement for Federal Express and one for Crest toothpaste have more in common with each other than the products/services or market environments for either of them.

That's why, when smart marketers need a positioning platform for a new product, they'll call in outside expertise in positioning, and do not try to do it themselves. Not only is it likely to be faster and more cost-efficient, but they'll probably get a better positioning statement to start with than if they tried to do it alone. And they know that the quality of the positioning statement is central to the entire marketing plan and the likely success of the new product. Certainly if you've ever been saddled with a less-than-ideal positioning you know how much it would have been worth to have gotten it right from the beginning. Changing an existing positioning is a very difficult process, much more so than creating it right in the first place.

The solution requires creative thinking

You may be getting a little tired of repeated references to creativity, insight, and intuition by now. The reason I bring them up here, though, is different from the reasons I've mentioned them before.

Most executives spend the bulk of their time, day-in and day-out, implementing projects and managing people. They have established routines and schedules that work for them, and they generally have appointments, meetings, conference calls, and items on their to-do lists that completely fill their daily calendars. They are in execution mode from the moment they set foot in the office until they leave at the end of the day, often burned out from the hectic routine into which they've fallen.

That's not a situation that's particularly conducive to creative thinking. There's a reason why people who are mostly "creative" don't have rigid schedules, don't have lots of people or projects vying for their attention, and don't have daily deadlines that stifle new thinking.

Consultants, by way of contrast to client executives, are creative. That is, they make their living by coming up with novel solutions to a client's problems and by turning on their "creative juices" (a/k/a intuition, insight, etc.) and applying them to the issues facing the client. They don't have the same kinds of pressures on them, so they're able to be more creative, devote more time thinking about the critical strategic issues, and come up with solutions that are almost certain to elude a busy, structured, over-scheduled client.

And consultants are not immersed in the complexities of the client's business, so they're better able to identify the right questions, address the most important issues, and guide the client to a better place than the client would have stumbled upon if left to his own devices. I can't tell you how many times we've been regarded as real heros by our clients simply because we were able to reframe the issues and define a new problem that struck at the real core of the situation. The clients couldn't do that because they were so intently focused on running the day-to-day business.

Clients recognize the advantages

When you put these three elements together – lack of time/ in-house expertise, the value of an outside perspective, and the creative climate – it's not hard to see why many companies, especially companies who recognize the value of sound strategic thinking, opt to use outside consultants on key projects. (You can quickly substitute the words that apply to your expertise, if it isn't strategic planning.)

The question you need to be asking is, "What does this mean for me as a consultant?"

If you are uncertain about your ability to deliver what your clients need and expect, then you may be in the wrong place as you assess the marketplace for your consulting services. If, on the other hand, you are salivating at the opportunity to put yourself on the line and commit to delivering against these basic client needs, then your notion of consulting may be exactly right for you.

It's NOT just about you and your needs. It's mostly about the clients' needs and your ability to satisfy them. If you're not looking at your decision through the clients' eyes now, what makes you think you'll be able to do so after you've jumped into the deep end of the consulting pool? And if you don't, you surely won't land and deliver the kinds of meaty, high-value projects that will assure your success as a consultant.

Chapter 8

The Most Common Client Misunderstandings

Having now laid out the most common reasons clients hire consultants, it's only fair that I share with you the most common client misperceptions about consulting. Unfortunately, I'm only able to speak of the ones I've encountered personally, and they're pretty specific to the kind of consulting I do – marketing and strategic planning. I'm going to share them anyway, because I suspect (a) you'll find them interesting in the absolute, and (b) you'll quickly begin to extend them into the kinds of questions or misperceptions that you'll likely face in whatever kind of consulting you decide to do.

Besides, there's a second level of importance for new consultants. Remember that you'll be marketing yourself to prospective clients, and your own perceptions and beliefs about marketing will impact your effectiveness as you do that. If you find that you are nodding in agreement with any of the myths below, you may want to adjust your own thinking about some of these marketing issues.

Widely-held myths about marketing (and marketing consulting)

If I've heard these once, I've heard them a hundred times. They're the comments that professional marketing consultants get from prospective clients almost every day. They aren't always explicit and direct, but after a while you recognize them regardless of the euphemisms, code-words, and disguises used to express them.

Here's my list of the top five:

1. *A great product sells itself.* We don't need marketing.
2. *We are already pretty good at marketing.* After all, we have the best sales force in the industry.
3. *We're in a commodity category.* The best marketing for us is a sharp pencil.
4. *Pricing is not a marketing issue.* Our finance people determine pricing strategy.
5. *Our business is unique.* If you don't have experience in our industry you probably can't help us.

As we go through each of these, you may want to consider the discussion from two different perspectives: (1) The equivalent myth(s) in your functional specialty, if it's not marketing; and (2) The way these misperceptions will affect your own efforts to market yourself as a consultant. (In the final analysis, we're all marketers.)

"A great product sells itself ... we don't need marketing"

Ever since the first person came up with the adage about building a better mousetrap ("and the world will beat a path to your door"), marketing has been a second-class citizen among most scientists and inventors. I've observed this phenomenon among artists (who think their works are so good they will sell themselves), product engineers (who are so excited about a technical achievement they forget that the hard work of marketing still lies ahead of them), lifelong entrepreneurs (who continually seek the next "sure-fire" product idea), and companies driven primarily by intense research and development.

Here's a perfect example: I recently had the opportunity to evaluate a small publishing business, owned and run by an author who had spent the last 30 years of his life writing more than three dozen terrific business books. He was reaching retirement age and wanted to sell the business.

Because he had put so much of his personal energy and time into creating the titles in his portfolio, he was convinced they were worth hundreds of thousands of dollars. "It would cost more than half a million dollars to recreate all of this," he said, and I don't question the accuracy of what he said, taken literally.

What he failed to appreciate is that in ten years the titles hardly generated enough adjusted net profit to cover the rent in his small office, let alone create real value in his business. He had all but ignored the marketing function, making an implicit assumption that if the content is good enough his titles should be worth a small fortune. He focused single-mindedly on putting great advice and suggestions into his books, writing in a clear and engaging manner, and ensuring that all the publishing and operations issues were properly addressed.

What he forgot was marketing. His books were not available in bookstores, through on-line booksellers, in catalogs, or through sales representatives who called on potential customers. He did no formal advertising and generated virtually no publicity. Even his website obscured the books (on web pages three or four levels deep), and that made it really challenging for a prospective buyer to order them. The only sales he had were generated by occasional calls to former consulting clients, and a few referral orders from speakers or seminar leaders who needed specific/customized versions of his books.

He tried to build a business solely on the quality of the product. What he learned is that a product-based business strategy is like a one-handed clap. Without marketing it's almost impossible to be noticed. And without demonstrated sales and profit it's almost impossible to sell a business for a significant multiple of earnings.

Apply this lesson to a consulting practice. No matter how good you are at your functional specialty, and no matter how much value you can bring to a prospective client, how will the client *know* about you and your capabilities if you don't market yourself? You'll want to guard against the temptation of thinking your resume or CV will do the job all by itself. You have to research your client, position yourself appropriately, and demonstrate your ability to address and solve the client's biggest problems. They're not likely to "discover" you all by themselves, regardless of your reputation, so you have to make yourself and your abilities relevant to them.

"We are already pretty good at marketing ... we have the best sales force in the industry"

Many clients confuse sales and marketing. They look at the combined sales-and-marketing function, call it "Marketing," but really think of it as "Sales." They just don't understand what the marketing function is or how it differs from sales.

To be sure, the marketing function *includes* sales, but it is much more than selling alone. It includes all the elements of the traditional marketing mix:

Positioning	Product/Offering
Pricing	Promotion
Packaging	Sales/Distribution
Advertising	Publicity

And there are additional layers of the marketing function that include such things as customer and consumer research, communication strategy, after-sale support, service, etc.

To confuse this function with "sales" is like confusing an automobile with its transmission. It is a critical component, but certainly not the same thing. (How far would you get without an engine, or tires, or a steering wheel, etc.?)

When I come across this misperception, I usually don't respond by telling the client he's wrong. Rather I try to build on the perception that the sales force is doing a great job, and raise the issue of how much more effective they'd be if they were supported by a strong marketing plan that includes all the other marketing mix elements. When possible, I point to examples in their industry (or industries with which they're familiar) and try to make my point with relevant case studies. That usually works.

When you consider your own consulting practice, the lesson is to create a comprehensive, written marketing plan for your business. Consider all the marketing mix elements, starting with positioning. It's not enough to just go out there and sell.

"We're in a commodity category ... the best marketing is a sharp pencil"

This is truly a self-defeating way to look at any business. If you believe your only differentiation is price – that you are truly a commodity – you're destined to fulfill your expectations and become one. Why you'd want that is beyond me.

This is not to say that all products have inherent product-based differentiation. I remember being brought into a consulting assignment for nylon carpet fiber – the stuff of which most broadloom carpet is made. As a consumer, you really can't tell the difference between fibers manufactured by different companies. Yet one company has been able to set itself apart from the others and actually command a significant price premium for a product that is impossible for the consumer to differentiate.

Similarly, when I used to work at Frito-Lay I was fascinated by the fact that two potatoes which looked alike to the naked eye could be peeled, sliced, fried, salted, and packaged in different bags, and end up appearing so different in consumers' eyes that more than 65% of potato chip buyers would strongly prefer one over the other.

My conclusion – and I know I'm not alone in this – is that there is really no such thing as a commodity. It's a defeatist mind-set on the part of the marketer, encouraged by professional purchasing agents who are rewarded by reducing everything to a price issue.

Incidentally, one tell-tale sign of a "commodity thinker" is preoccupation with competitors' actions and pricing moves. When a client constantly refers to what competitors are doing (as a basis for what he should be doing), I begin to suspect the commodity mentality. It usually doesn't take too many follow-up questions to verify my suspicions.

In one case I was able to prove my point by taking the client through an exercise in which the management team estimated the likely volume/share impact of different competitive actions. I was able to demonstrate that their own estimates would make their planned competitive response less profitable than doing nothing at all, or even doing the opposite of their knee-jerk reaction.

From a consultant's perspective, if you view yourself as a commodity – "just another consultant" – you're essentially selling your time, not your best thinking. As such, you're an hourly or piece-work laborer, subject to supply-and-demand economics. In short, you are a commodity.

I submit that you would be much better served finding a project where your expertise, experience, training, knowledge, and demonstrated abilities are truly unique and represent a targeted solution to the client's problems. That way you'll have something to sell that keeps you out of the commodity – and piece-work – category. And it will probably allow you to command a premium price for your services.

"Pricing is not a marketing issue"

A surprising number of companies view pricing strategy as a way to recover costs and earn profit. Of course, there's nothing wrong with recovering costs and earning profit, but if that's how you view pricing, you're probably not optimizing your marketing effort. Pricing is part of the marketing mix, and it needs to be consistent with, and supportive of, the positioning and overall strategy.

A more appropriate view of pricing, I would submit, is that it's the ultimate expression of the value of a company's offering. If you have a superior product, why would you price it like a private label brand? And if you have an unbranded, undifferentiated product, what would make you think you could get top dollar for it?

And when we refer to the "product," we really should refer to the total product offering. Consumers have always and consistently demonstrated that they prefer to pay a premium price to get products and services ("offerings") they perceive to be superior. It's true in computers (where after-sale support, bundled software, features, delivery, etc. are all part of the offering); clothing (where style, fit, brand-name/logo, durability, comfort, and returnability are all part of the offering); overnight delivery services (where the assurance that it's "absolutely, positively" *guaranteed* to show up the next day is part of the offering); and just about every other product or service category.

People don't just buy products (or services) for the lowest possible price. They buy value – the sum-total of what they feel they receive compared to what they have to pay. And they'll almost always consider the benefits as their highest priority, not the cost.

The lesson for a consultant is that low fees aren't the only – or best – way to land a new client or project. Low fees suggest low quality. Is that the way you want to be perceived? If so, I'd like the opportunity to compete against you for the next consulting project. (My goal is usually to propose a project with a fee that's HIGHER than everyone else, so that I have the opportunity to explain why I'm the client's best value. I walk away from clients who make their selections solely based on the lowest fee.)

"Our business is unique"

Many clients are convinced that if you haven't spent years and years in their industry you can't possibly bring value to their business. They make "industry experience" a prerequisite for every hire – whether as an employee or a consultant.

Of course, literally speaking, every business IS unique, but every business is also a business, and someone who is truly knowledgeable and skilled in business can be considered expert at some level. The same is true for marketing, sales, finance, investment banking, human resources, business law, and many/most other functions. A client who rejects help from an expert in an area in which his company is lagging is missing the point when he insists on "industry experience."

The misperception that only someone with industry experience can help has actually proven to be a great selling point for me in my own consulting business. I invite prospective clients to consider that industry experience also implies industry "baggage," and suggest that someone with a fresh outside perspective might actually be more appropriate – as long as they can learn enough about the industry quickly enough to make the appropriate leaps and draw useful parallels from experience in other industries.

I then tell them about projects I've successfully delivered in such diverse industries as agricultural and industrial chemicals, fibers, apparel, computer hardware and software, consumer durable goods (like major household appliances, for example), consumer packaged goods (both food and non-food), business-to-business services, construction material (engineered wood products, thermal insulation, etc.), ingredient products, healthcare services (including high-tech diagnostic equipment, consumables and insurance), financial products and services, and a host of others.

I explain that they'll be ahead of the curve if they retain a credentialed expert in marketing strategy (with a successful track record across many industries) who can quickly learn about their industry, rather than trying to find a [banker, farmer, hospital administrator, scientist, engineer … whatever] who is also an expert in marketing strategy. It doesn't usually take too long to convince them this is correct, and I quickly offer referrals to my clients who had initially thought the same way and who later came to appreciate that they were wrong.

Chapter 9

Consulting Between Jobs

If you now understand the seven personal characteristics, what a consultant's life is like, the consulting proposal, the importance of understanding client needs, and how clients view consultants and consulting relationships, the answer to the question "Am I well suited to being a consultant?" lies in the fit between your own interests, style, wants and needs, and the "requirements" for being a successful consultant.

You need to be honest with yourself, of course, or you're only setting the stage for inevitable failure. You'll probably want to gain some perspective from people who know you well – family members, friends, business colleagues, etc. – and perhaps an objective career counselor with no axe to grind. If you know someone who has preceded you in the move from your prior career into consulting, you'll want to talk with him or her too. Ask the tough questions, because you'll be living with your decision for quite a while, whether you're successful or not. Your decision to consult is arguably one of the most important you'll ever make.

Clearly this is a critically important career decision, and it shouldn't be made under duress or as a knee-jerk reaction to not having any other good options. A mistake here will not only make you miserable for the few months or years you're consulting, but it can throw a permanent monkey wrench into your long-term career strategy and make the next transition all the more difficult and painful.

I'm not trying to talk you out of consulting. I'm just trying to maintain an objective view of the situation – of your goals, your strategies, your values, and your lifestyle. What does success look like for you? Are you focused on your own best interests over the long haul, or are you preoccupied with solving a short-term problem as quickly as possible?

Should consulting be part of your job search strategy?

What about consulting WHILE you're looking for your next real career move? Is that a good idea or a bad one? Let's start by considering some of the reasons you might want to consult while you're in transition:

- First, it keeps you "in the loop" as far as your industry and professional contacts are concerned. You remain "part of the fraternity" and stay current on all the news, gossip, and latest developments because you're still a player – even if it's in a limited or temporary capacity. And perhaps someone at your client company could even become a reference when the consulting assignment is finished and you're back in the job market.

- Next, and not to be minimized, it brings in some cash. That's important when you don't have a regular paycheck coming in every month.

- And, of course, it gives you something productive to do, gets you out of the house, and sidesteps any possible personal conflicts at home. It actually *feels* like real work – and it keeps your mind off the stress you've been dealing with for however many months it's been since you found yourself in the job market.

- And then there's the dream that maybe – just maybe – the consulting assignment will lead to a perfect permanent, full-time position, and you'll end up solving your real problem – getting the job you want.

Overall, these sound like reasonable benefits, and worth serious consideration, don't they? Let's look at the flip side of this coin before you become too eager to hang out a consulting shingle:

- Perhaps the most important issue is whether you really have the skill set and temperament to be a good consultant. Maybe you do and maybe you don't. And if you don't, you could end up doing your career a real disservice by demonstrating your ineptness to a prospective employer and colleagues in the industry.

- Second, consulting is hard work and requires a certain kind of personal make-up that most people who work for larger companies (or even smaller ones) don't always have. You have to be able to learn very quickly, trust your intuition, perform flawlessly virtually all the time, and really understand not only the specific business issues or problems facing your client, but also the corporate climate, politics, and norms in your temporary workplace.

- Third, you don't have the luxury of crawling up the learning curve, establishing long-term relationships with co-workers based on a history of trust, or assimilating into the culture over a period of months or years. You're expected to contribute immediately and perform at a level that no "regular employee" could possibly sustain. That's pressure.

- And while you're giving that assignment your all, how much time do you think you'll have to devote to the research and leg-work necessary to find a permanent job? How many hours a day can you work effectively?

- Next, consider that most companies don't give the plum assignments to temporary consultants – especially consultants who are obviously between jobs. Chances are you'll be doing work that doesn't utilize all your skills, is not particularly challenging for you, and does little or nothing to really build your value to the next employer. Is it worth the detour on your career path? Is this really consulting, or are you simply selling a few hours or days of your time?

- And remember the dream about the consulting assignment turning into the permanent, full-time job you really wanted all along? Don't count on it. In my opinion and experience, you're better off buying a lottery ticket. I know a few people who consulted for a while, then found a company that wanted to hire them. But it wasn't the company they had as a client. Turning a client into an employer is very rare – especially if you're viewed as a temporary consultant to begin with.

Net, I believe that for most executives consulting is not a great way to keep busy when you're between jobs. It's possible you're an exception, but you need to be hard on yourself when you're making this decision. You need to be very sure you're not just reacting to relieve your short-term pain, without consideration of the longer-term implications or the inevitable delay in finding the job you really want.

And you have to be sure that you are not setting yourself up for disappointment when it finally sinks in that you're not going to be calling the shots as a consultant the same way you did as a line manager.

The steps to consulting between jobs

Let's assume that you've considered all the pros and cons, and that you've decided to at least TRY consulting while the opportunity seems right. You've always thought the lifestyle looked attractive – and you can really use the extra income, even if it does delay your real career progress a few months.

How do you land a consulting assignment? Interestingly, the first few steps are exactly the same as those you might take if you were looking for a "real" job.

- First, you lay out a clear positioning and marketing strategy for yourself/your consulting business (or your job search). And be sure it's written down, not just "in your head." There's something almost magical about committing yourself in writing, and it almost always forces you to think things through more thoroughly.

- Then you do the deep-dive research to find the perfect prospective client (or employer) – perhaps spending as much as a month or two doing your homework before you even approach the prospect.

- Then you identify and contact people who can give you additional information and perhaps provide an introduction to the right people at the client company (or future employer).

- Of course, once you actually make your presentation (or secure an interview), you need to level with the client-to-be (or prospective employer) and tell them what you're doing and why. You have to be yourself, because they'll figure it out soon enough anyway, and if you've lied to them you'll be worse off than if you'd stayed home and done nothing.

Given that these are all the same steps you'd be going through if you were considering a full-time permanent job, you're probably asking yourself at this point, "If I have to go to all this trouble to land a *temporary* consulting assignment, why wouldn't I shoot for the permanent position I really want? It's the same amount of work, the same preparation, the same networking, and the same basic story. Why do all of that for a short-term return when I can have a long-term one instead?"

That's a good question, and it's one of the reasons I conclude that for most executives consulting between jobs is not the best use of time and energy. Of course, this entire discussion was prefaced with the presumption that you really wanted to try consulting, and that you didn't have any other, more attractive, options or alternatives competing for your time and attention.

Still interested?

If you you are now convinced that consulting is right for you as a between-jobs activity, or that it is the perfect strategy for landing your next job, then I'd urge you to put your marketing hat on, go through all the steps we've discussed about strategic planning for yourself, and then try your hand at consulting even before you approach a client. **Do the project that will convince them they need you, and see if it lands the assignment.**

If it does, then maybe it was a good idea. If not, then you've tested the water without diving into the deep end too quickly or too publicly.

The up-front mini-project is the approach that has proven most effective for me in my own consulting practice, and it's the one recommended by every professional (and successful) consultant I've interviewed. You'll know soon enough if you have what it takes and if it's what you really want to be doing – even on an interim basis. Chances are you won't get a good consulting assignment any other way, so you really have nothing to lose by trying it.

And who knows? It could end up as the first link in a chain of events that lands you right where you wanted to be in the first place.

This is a low-risk way to "sample" consulting, and you are virtually guaranteed to end up with experience and knowledge you wouldn't have had if you hadn't tried it.

Another alternative for job seekers

If you are unsure about your suitability for consulting (and vice versa), and what you really want is to feel productive and demonstrate your strong work ethic, commitment, and skill set, let me suggest an alternative that will satisfy all of those needs.

Find a volunteer opportunity and give back to your community while you have the opportunity. It does wonders for your own state of mind, and it taps into a kinder, gentler, more altruistic aspcet of yourself.

Nobody on his death bed ever said "I wish I'd spent more time at the office," but a lot of people regret that they never took the time and made the effort to help others less fortunate than themselves.

Volunteering this way not only satisfies that higher place in yourself, but it often turns into a wonderful talking point in an interview, gives you life experiences, insights, and new skills you'd never get any other way. And it reminds you every day that your problems are small compared to those facing a lot of other folks.

If you really have the itch to do something worthwhile while you're in transition, that's what I'd recommend. Everyone who has tried it becomes an evangelist, so there must be something to it.

Chapter 10

The Five Keys to Consulting Success

At this point we've considered all the reasons you might want to try consulting, and now it's my job is to give you the information that will help you succeed in your new career.

I believe there are five important keys to success in consulting. They're necessary and sufficient, and they've been tested and proven by hundreds, if not thousands, of consultants before you and me. They apply regardless of the kind of consulting you want to do, and they should all be taken VERY seriously.

I'd only qualify them by reminding you that the consulting we are talking about is not simply selling your time on an hourly or per-diem basis, or serving as a contract employee for a short period of time. It's providing advice, know-how, expertise, and/or creative thinking that clients will find valuable. It's about helping them achieve their objectives, and being seen as a profit generator, not an incremental (and burdensome) cost.

I'm assuming you already have experience and skills that clients will find valuable, that you understand the lifestyle implications, and that you've been through the prerequisites and considerations laid out earlier in this book. Having taken all that into consideration, you are now ready to jump in and become a consultant.

With that as an introduction, here are the five keys to consulting success:

1. **Set realistic client expectations up-front and plan to over-deliver on every project.**

2. **Develop and communicate a clear positioning for yourself.**

3. **Plan your own marketing strategy as thoroughly and carefully as you would the client's project.**

4. **Do your homework.**

5. **Set and maintain the highest standards of personal and professional integrity.**

Because these five keys are so important, each bears some focused discussion.

Set realistic client expectations up-front and plan to over-deliver on every project

Every successful consultant will tell you that it's a whole lot easier to get another project assignment from a satisfied client than it is to find a new client and land an initial assignment. If you've done a good job on the first project, the client already knows he can count on you and is obviously convinced that the common misperceptions about consultants (generally) are not true.

What isn't quite so obvious – especially to new consultants – is that a project's success is usually determined before the proposal is even submitted, and certainly before the initial start-up meeting. This might sound strange if you've never been a consultant, but it won't take you long to fully appreciate its importance after you've delivered a few projects and tried to sell a few new projects.

The reason the project's success is predetermined is that "success" is in the client's eyes, not judged by some outside "project police." If the client expects 70 (on some internal and indefinable scale of satisfaction) and you deliver 65, they're going to feel like they didn't quite get their money's worth. If they feel like you only delivered 50, they might even refuse to pay the fee. And the scoring is all in the client's perception, not some objective measure.

On the other hand, if the client feels you delivered 75 or 80, he's going to feel like he got more than he bargained for, and you'll be seen as having over-delivered on the project. That's where you want to be. You'll be rewarded for your over-delivery, if not immediately then soon afterward.

So the question is, "How does the client set his expectation level?" If you can affect that, you have an excellent chance of exceeding expectations and giving the client everything he wanted – and more.

The answer to that question, fortunately, is that the client's expectations are almost entirely in the consultant's control! The client's expectations are set when the consultant presents the initial proposal. If the proposal exaggerates the deliverable, then the client has every reason (and right) to expect an exaggerated deliverable. If the proposal is more modest, and explains clearly what will be included in the deliverable, and what won't be included, then the client will be pleasantly surprised if and when the consultant delivers more than promised.

The end is determined before the project even begins!

And why do most consultants miss this point? Because they are so eager to land the project that they promise the moon, and stars, and a few comets for good measure. They propose the project they WISH they could deliver, without understanding that they're working against their own long-term success.

The amateur psychologist in me hypothesizes that they're feeling a little insecure, or vulnerable, and they think that if they promise more there's a better chance they'll get the project. They're focused on winning the contract, not on delivering the project. Or they're not realistic about their own ability to deliver.

In any event, they're virtually guaranteeing that the relationship will be less than satisfactory in the client's eyes, and they're sealing their fate for future projects with that client.

The best strategy, I've found, is to under-promise and over-deliver. And to do it consistently, according to plan. Set the bar at a level you're sure you can clear, and then clear it comfortably and easily. If you're not sure you can clear the bar, don't even bid on the project, because you'll only live to regret it.

Of course, "setting the bar" with a new client is something of an art form that gets easier as you gain consulting experience. You not only get to know your own capabilities better, but you also gain additional insight into clients' thinking and how they express their needs. The first few times it's a little scary (though that doesn't make it any less critical).

If you view consulting as a form of teaching, you may have a leg up in the expectation-setting phase of a project. That's been my approach.

It's your job to teach your prospective client what to expect and why that's appropriate. If you do a good job, and the client trusts your "lesson," you can anticipate a realistic expectation. If you don't, there's a good chance you either don't have a good grasp on the situation yourself, or are not being realistic about your ability to deliver. Either way there's a problem, and it should be addressed before you get yourself into real consulting trouble.

Develop and communicate a clear positioning for yourself

Positioning is what the customer thinks in the deep recesses of his consciousness when your name comes up. Don't make the mistake of thinking it's something you tell him. You might be able to influence his perceptions, but only he knows what goes on in his own mind.

If you say all the right words and make all the right points about yourself, but you forget to zip your pants before you present, there's a good chance that the first thing the client will remember when your name comes up is "the guy whose fly wasn't closed." That's your positioning. (Women can draw their own parallels – an unbuttoned blouse, a too-short skirt, etc.) Of course, the thing people remember about you doesn't have to be related just to your appearance. I've used those examples because they're so easy to visualize.

With that in mind, the challenge is to develop a clear and effective positioning platform and to communicate it as effectively as possible. You'll know you've been successful when the client's feedback is consistent with your intended communication.

I've had this experience a few times when a client recommended me to a colleague and the colleague began our conversation with "Bob suggested I give you a call. He said you were an insightful consultant who over-delivers with creative approaches on marketing strategy projects."

I knew when I heard that introduction that Bob got my intended positioning. I'd presented myself effectively to him and reinforced the positioning when I delivered his project.

I have developed an entire workshop on the subject of Positioning, but I don't want this to turn into a treatise on that subject, so let me give you a simple example that I think makes the main point:

> Imagine that you are the owner of a bakery that makes terrific cakes – chocolate, angel food, lemon, spice, carrot, and all sorts of specialty flavors and styles. You could position yourself, like a bakery near my office has, as "Great Cakes." That should appeal to just about everyone who likes cake.

> Now suppose 100% of your customers only buy one kind of cake – say, chocolate. Would you still position yourself as Great Cakes? Of course not. You'd position yourself to appeal to what your customers want – Great Chocolate Cake. There's no reason to try to convince people who want chocolate that they shouldn't want it. And there's no reason to position and advertise yourself as something they obviously don't want.

The same is true for positioning yourself as a consultant. If you know what your prospective client wants, there's no reason to ramble on about how good you are at something else. Give the client the information he's seeking – and position yourself as the person who can best deliver that benefit. It's that simple – and that important.

If there's a place that most businesses fail, it's in the up-front positioning. People, for some reason, don't fully understand and appreciate positioning, so they don't give it the attention it deserves. It's only when something else doesn't work the way they want it to that they realize where the problem originated, and then it's usually too late to take corrective action. Remember, positioning is what's in the client's mind, not what you think it should be.

* * * * *

In Appendix C there's a recap of key points from my Positioning workshop, including the requirements for a good positioning statement, and I'd urge you to review it if you plan to develop a positioning statement for yourself and your consulting business.

Plan your own marketing strategy as thoroughly and carefully as you would the client's project

As you develop your positioning and marketing strategy, keep in mind that you are essentially setting up a demonstration for your client. You'll be demonstrating how seriously you take your professional life, how clearly you think and communicate, and what they can expect from you in a possible consulting relationship. It's hard for me to understand why anyone would present himself to a prospective client without having gone through this process, but I know many do. My guess is they're the ones who don't land too many projects.

I usually use the checklist of marketing mix elements to be sure I've covered all the bases and thought through all the aspects of marketing myself before a client presentation:

Positioning	*Product/Offering*
Pricing	*Packaging*
Publicity	*Promotion*
Sales/Distribution	*Advertising*

Positioning has been covered in the previous point. It's clearly the single most important component of the marketing mix because it provides the foundation for everything else. Besides, if a client doesn't understand the positioning it's unlikely he'll understand the other elements and how they relate to each other.

Product/Offering is the deliverable. What should the client expect from you in the final analysis? What is the "essential DNA" of what you offer? Product is a marketing mix element because if your offering isn't what clients need and want, then you either have to change it or find other clients – clients whose needs you can satisfy. (We'll be talking about researching and identifying client needs very soon.)

Pricing is your fee, payment terms, any extras or add-ons, and what the total cost to the client is going to be. If it's not in line with the perceived value of the benefits, you probably won't get the project. Challenge yourself to calculate a dollar value for the benefits the client should expect and compare that value to your fee. Is this a win-win proposition, or is the fee out of line? And be sure you're fair to yourself, too. When I first started consulting I consistently priced my services at what I thought was a fair price, only to kick myself when the project expanded beyond the scope I had in my mind, or ran a month longer than I'd expected, etc.

Packaging is the physical trapping of your offering. If you're writing your proposal on company letterhead, does it reflect the positioning? If you're delivering a formal report, do the binding and organization say as much about the quality of your work as does the content? Does your business card communicate not only the requisite contact information but also the right image? How about your clothes, your demeanor, and your attitude? And your e-mail address: is it professional or is it *Cutiepie23@aol.com*? What about your answering machine or voice mail messages: are they professional? All of these things are part of your offering; they're your "packaging," and they can make or break the communication of your positioning.

Publicity is the way people learn about you – the "buzz on the street" when it comes to your niche in consulting. You'll probably want to manage publicity carefully, especially when you're first getting started. You may want to send a news release to the relevant trade press, or create a brochure you can leave with clients. And you'll almost certainly want a website they can visit to learn more about your positioning, product or service offering, client list, etc. And they'll use it to compare you to others they may be considering. Publicity is closely related to advertising and promotion.

Promotion overlaps somewhat with publicity in that its intent is to get the word out, create awareness of you and your positioning, and to generate some level of interest prior to a sales call. It goes beyond that, though, because it is more focused on generating an immediate sale. You might consider a "free trial size" of your services, specific to the client's needs. That's been a very effective tool not only for consumer packaged goods but for just about every product or service – including consulting. The thing you want to avoid is a "price" promotion in which you discount your services.

Sales/Distribution is the function that establishes and maintains a strong, positive client relationship and ensures that the product actually makes it to the customer as promised. It's also the function that prepares the proposal, sets appropriate client expectations, and ensures that the deliverable exceeds those expectations. In a small company – when you're working alone – the sales function is almost indistinguishable from all the other marketing mix elements; they are all focused on strengthening client relationships, delivering in a way that exceeds expectations, and setting the stage for landing the next project.

Ongoing customer service is a close cousin to – and maybe even part of – Sales. It's important because it directly impacts the client relationship and client satisfaction. The difference is that it isn't quite so focused on immediate needs (i.e., closing the sale) and may not even involve the primary decision-maker.

Advertising is the overt, awareness-generating communication that you send out to prospective customers. It can be in the form of mass communication – like broadcast or print media – or it can be direct mail, e-mail, matchbook covers, fliers, or any number of other approaches.

For large companies serving mass markets, advertising often consumes the lion's share of the marketing budget. In smaller companies, a well-planned website might be the extent of a company's advertising. The important consideration is that the advertising needs to communicate the positioning in a clear, direct way, so that everyone who sees or hears it will be sure to notice it, get the big idea, and understand what you're all about. Don't dismiss advertising too quickly if you're not a big company, though, as there are many inexpensive approaches that have proven to be quite effective.

Many times advertising and publicity are considered together because they share a common objective – creating awareness of the company and its positioning. The difference is that advertising content is completely controlled by the company, while publicity is more word-of-mouth and subject to a wide range of different interpretations (or "spin") as it gets further from the source.

I'm not suggesting with this discussion of marketing mix components that you are or should be a big company with multiple departments and sub-specialists on staff. I'm simply listing and defining the key elements because each of them is likely to come into play as you plan your presentations, and you'll want to give them all serious thought before you first set foot in the client's office.

Do your homework

In my view, the essence of marketing and consulting is the identification of actionable insight. Once you have the insight, solving the problem is usually relatively easy.

Before you can begin to search for the understanding that will lead to a solution of a client's problem, though, you have to be sure you are asking the right questions. If your understanding is different from the client's, then you'll probably be addressing a different (i.e., the wrong) issue. No client is likely to retain you to solve a problem he doesn't think he has, and it doesn't matter whether the problem you've identified is really the right one or not.

So the whole process actually begins with homework. Homework in many cases is synonymous with research, because it's "looking into" a situation that gives us the fodder for coming up with insight. And if you are naturally curious, the homework can actually be fun. I personally enjoy this phase of a project most, because it gives me a chance to create real value just by applying my own novel thinking.

I've made the point before that selecting the right client is the first step in a successful consulting project. If you find the client whose biggest, most important problem can be solved by whatever it is you do best, you've got the makings of a terrific consulting relationship. It's a marriage made in heaven, so to speak. That's another reason why the up-front research, or homework, is so important. You don't want to spend your time on potential clients whose needs don't fall in your area of unique skill and expertise. It takes the same amount of time and effort to research the RIGHT client as the WRONG one.

And all of this leads us to the hot, new topic of TMI, or Too Much Information, which some management theorists would have us believe can obscure important issues and lead us down inappropriate blind alleys in our search for solutions.

While I understand their point and appreciate the potential for being buried in wrong or misleading information, it seems to me that this is rarely a problem for good consultants who have an instinct for separating the wheat from the chaff when it comes to client input and finding "truth" in a situation analysis. More often the problem is NEI (Not Enough Information) and a gap in understanding that can lead to a misdiagnosis of the problem and/ or an unworkable solution.

Clearly there is an appropriate middle ground, and it's been my observation that the TMI problem is a much smaller risk than NEI. If you have a critical, analytical approach to problem solving, you're almost always better off doing more up-front research. And having all the extra data to stimulate your creative thinking process can only help generate a broader range of possible solutions.

We sometimes refer to this important stage of a project as "doing the deep dive," because we want to thoroughly understand all the nuances and implications of what we learn, so that we can frame the question(s) in a way that will address the client's real needs.

Set and maintain the highest standards of personal and professional integrity

I would hope that this final point is so obvious that no one will actually challenge it. After all, you wouldn't want to be known as someone who has anything less than high standards, would you?

Yet many people who have tried consulting and returned to the client side feel that they had to compromise their own ethical standards in consulting and didn't like having to do that in order to make a decent living. Let me offer one example:

I mentioned earlier that almost every consultant knows it's a lot easier to sell another project to a current client than it is to identify and sell a new client on using your services. That means you're always scouting new opportunities as you're working on an existing client's project. It's not something you necessarily do consciously; it just happens. You're there, you're talking with people who know the business, you're sensitized to spot opportunities, and you're involved in the issues that affect the client company in a lot of ways. You'd almost be remiss if you didn't notice them.

Whether you find that kind of "inside prospecting" ethical or not is probably open to some question or debate. Some of you will and some of you won't. I know one former consultant found that kind of behavior repulsive (and unavoidable), and it soured him on consulting as a career or way of life. I know others who believe it's natural, expected, and desirable to be looking for additional ways to help your client, and actually feel they're doing exactly the right thing to be scouting new business this way.

I'm not going to take sides on this issue because that's not the point. The point is that if you are not determined to live up to the highest standards of personal and professional integrity in your consulting practice you're going to have a tough time looking at yourself in the mirror every morning, and you need to ask yourself the hard questions BEFORE you make the commitment. Don't get blind-sided by an ethics issue AFTER you've made the decision to consult.

There's an additional reason why integrity should matter to you. Consultants live by their reputations. Any consultant who has betrayed a confidence or exhibited questionable professional behavior quickly finds that "the word is out," and virtually every client prospect is leery of hiring that consultant. Clients don't spend large sums of money (like consulting fees, for example) without checking references and doing their own homework. If you have even the hint of inappropriate behavior lurking in your background, it's going to become known before long, and you'll find that landing a new consulting assignment is almost impossible. I've seen it happen, and it's not pretty.

There's an organization called The Institute of Management Consultants. It has a number of local chapters, an international affiliation, and a formal code of ethics which all members must agree to uphold. (For the record, the organization's Mission Statement and the Code of Ethics can be found in Appendix D.)

The reason I mention it specifically is that there's a phrase in the Code of Ethics that says members voluntarily pledge to assume "self-discipline above and beyond the requirements of law." That gets at the idea pretty well. It means an honorable consultant does more than simply follow the specific "thou shalt" and "thou shalt not" guidelines listed in the code – all thirteen of them. It means you have to embrace the highest ethical standards possible, and it has to come from within.

Consultants are entrusted with an almost sacred responsibility – the care and nurturing of the stockholders' "baby" – and they must always remember that they fill that role, even if it was never made explicit. (Remember how Rasputin got his start in consulting!)

This critical success factor is listed last, but it's the first one that can disqualify you if you don't take it seriously. It's a knock-out punch unlike any other – especially for consultants in a highly competitive marketplace.

Chapter 11

Recapping the Lessons From Rasputin

At the beginning of this book we identified 26 lessons from "The Story of a Successful Consultant." You'll remember that the hero of our story in Chapter 1, Greg, was a present-day surrogate for Grigori Yefimovich Rasputin, "The Evil Monk" in Russian history and perhaps the most infamous consultant ever.

In the subsequent chapters we reviewed several aspects of consulting – basic requirements, the consulting project and proposal, client attitudes, marketing, and critical success factors.

In the course of the discussions, we actually covered all 26 of the lessons learned from Greg (and, indirectly, from Rasputin himself). What we'll do now is review the story paragraph-by-paragraph and recap the lessons of importance to would-be consultants. In each case, we've also included specific reference or two to the pages on which each topic was covered in this book. If you've forgotten something, or if it doesn't look familiar, just flip back to the pages on which the subject was covered and you'll be able to refresh your memory and lock in the lesson.

The Story of a Successful Consultant
– one lesson at a time

Greg didn't have a graduate degree or a resume that was particularly impressive, but he had learned some valuable skills and understood enough about the fundamentals of consulting to achieve what many would consider a stellar level of success in his chosen profession. He'd traveled a bit, seen a number of professionals in action, and he was astute enough to learn from them. He was a quick study, insightful analyst, and effective communicator.

Lesson 1: Formal education isn't nearly as important as having useful, marketable skills.

What clients care about is how quickly and effectively you can solve their problems. They don't care where or if you went to college, what your major was, whether you have an MBA, or even whether you graduated from high school. Your past accomplishments and education may be important to you, but what's important to a client is whether or not you can solve his problem. Be sure you focus on what's important to the client when you're selling a project. It's all about them, not about you.

For more detialed discussion of this lesson, see pages 90-92.

Lesson 2: You can learn by observing others, as long as (a) they're the right people, and (b) you know what to watch for/learn from them.

Everything you say or do as a consultant doesn't have to be original. It just has to solve the client's problem. Of course, solutions that you come up with yourself will make you feel good, and there's nothing wrong with that. Just don't let your needs overshadow the client's needs. Watching and learning from successful consultants, clients, or industry experts is a great way to build up your own skill set.

For more detialed discussion of this lesson, see pages 42-46.

Lesson 3: Critical skills: quick study, insightful analysis, effective communicator.

Everyone we contacted for input about the required skills for consultants came up with these three. There are lots of ways to look at them, and even more ways to express the ideas, but at their core, the three things every successful consultant must exhibit are (1) an ability to grasp the situation and its implications quickly, (2) the ability to draw actionable conclusions from insightful independent analysis, and (3) dynamite communication skills – listening, reading body language, asking penetrating questions, writing clearly and persuasively, teaching, speaking, telling stories, and giving stand-up presentations complete with visual aids, demonstrations, and examples.

For more detialed discussion of this lesson, see pages 42-49.

Shortly after returning from one of his trips, Greg found himself out of work, with no money and in need of some cash to fund his next venture. He was also astute enough to recognize that the real key to leveraging his skills was to find an employer who really needed what he did, and bill not for his time but for his know-how. He needed to capture the full value of his deliverable to the client, not just rent himself out by the hour or the day.

Lesson 4: Key is finding the right client.

It's more important to find a client whose biggest problem can be solved by what you do best than it is to tell the world how good you are at everything. Consulting is all about finding the right problems to solve, not telling people how many different things you can do.

For more detailed discussion of this lesson, see pages 68-69 and 136.

Lesson 5: Bill for what you deliver; focus on the benefit, not on how many hours/days it will take you to do the job. (Clients value what they pay for and pay for what they value.)

Charging for value delivered is a much smarter way to price your consulting services than simply selling hours or days. It forces you to face the real issue — what value you bring to the client's business situation — and it keeps the client focused on the result, or benefit, not on the process. Clients, like consumers in virtually every product category, actually prefer to pay more for greater value received.

For more detailed discussion of this lesson, see pages 93-97.

Instead of poring through the classified ads or going door-to-door asking for work, Greg embarked on an in-depth research project to find a potential employer whose greatest need was precisely what Greg knew how to do best. It took a bit of digging, and a few months of hard work, but he eventually found the situation he knew would be perfect for his needs — the ideal consulting gig, if he could land it.

Lesson 6: Consulting jobs don't find you; you find them.

If you hang out your shingle and wait for clients to discover how smart you are, you will have a lonely life. You have to market your services, just like just everyone else. And consulting is a service category where advertising in mass media doesn't usually pay off. You need to carefully define the ideal client, or problem you can solve best, and then search for the customer that fits that profile. It's a highly targeted marketing process, not a shotgun approach.

For more detailed discussion of this lesson, see pages 68 and 108-110.

Lesson 7: It's not a numbers game.

Don't think that a mass mailing of several hundred letters to every company in sight is going to land even one solid consulting assignment. It doesn't work that way. You'll be much more effective at landing a project if you focus on the one company that needs you most. (Rasputin only needed one parent of a hemophiliac child to build his consulting practice!)

For more detailed discussion of this lesson, see page 68.

Lesson 8: Research is the most important element in landing a consulting project, and it's all done up-front. (This also applies to a job search, of course.)

The better you understand a client's situation, the better your chances of landing a consulting project will be. Don't be afraid to invest a considerable amount of time and money learning everything you can before you present yourself to a client. They'll appreciate the effort you made, and you'll be offering what they really want and need.

For more detailed discussion of this lesson, see pages 66-69, 122, and 135-137.

Lesson 9: Identify a project you can master.

A consultant's reputation is directly related to how well he did on his most recent assignment. Don't risk damage to your own reputation by grabbing a project that you can't deliver with flying colors. You'll only live to regret it, no matter how much you need the work right now.

For more detailed discussion of this lesson, see pages 40, 111-113, and 136.

He developed a strategy that he'd seen work many times before. He began to network with individuals who might know key people at the target client. He was still in research mode, and he learned even more about the client from his contacts. It seems the client was in over his head. The job was terribly complex, and there were so many pieces to manage that it was impossible to set and stick to priorities. Besides, the client wasn't really cut out for the job to begin with. To make matters worse, the number two person was preoccupied with other matters, and the internal staff simply didn't have the skills or know-how to deal with the seemingly unsolvable problems.

Lesson 10: Networking is primarily a research tool.

You can't count on others to do your marketing for you. That's not what networking is all about. Think of networking as information gathering or research, not as begging for assistance. If you can convert a casual contact into an introduction vehicle (to your next client), that's a bonus.

For more detailed discussion of this lesson, see page 122.

Lesson 11: Consulting works best when you have skills the client doesn't have.

If the client had the necessary skills and time, he wouldn't need an outside consultant. Your highest value to a prospective client is applying your unique skill set and experience to his problem and coming up with a workable solution.

For more detailed discussion of this lesson, see pages 90-92 and 100-101.

It didn't take long before Greg had an action plan and was ready to implement. He secured the introductions he needed. He would "work his magic" to solve Number Two's biggest problem, thus establishing a credential that would earn him the trust and appreciation of everyone on the client team.

Lesson 12: Strategic planning comes first; then implementation.

Don't fall into the ready-fire-aim syndrome. It's tempting to get out there and sell – paticularly to generate some revenue. Unfortunately, most turn-downs and rejections occur when you haven't first done your homework, developed a strategy, and planned your approach. Put strategy first on your priority list and you'll find that your batting average increases much faster that way.

For more detailed discussion of this lesson, see pages 57-58 and 131-135..

Lesson 13: Consider the client individuals/team, not just the business issues.

Clients are people too. They have individual needs, department needs, company needs, and interpersonal relationships in which they've invested a lot of time and energy. Be sensitive to them, and deliver more than a great business solution.

For more detailed discussion of this lesson, see pages 57-58 and 71.

When the time came, it worked just as Greg had planned it. Number Two agreed to meet with him based on referrals from his networking contacts. He committed to solving Number Two's biggest single problem, in return for a nice consulting fee and an introduction to the Big Boss. The price he set was high considering the time and effort involved, but quite reasonable when you considered the benefits for the client. And there didn't seem to be any viable alternative, so he was not really competing on a price basis anyway.

Lesson 14: Pre-play all important meetings: "What's the best thing that can happen at this meeting?"

Role-playing each client interaction in your mind before opening your mouth will pay off more than all the dress rehearsals in front of a mirror. Figure out in advance what you'd like to have happen at a meeting and watch how often you get your wish. You'll wonder how it happens so often, and why you didn't do this years ago.

For more detailed discussion of this lesson, see pages 50-51.

Lesson 15: Keep it simple stupid. (KISS)

Boil everything down to the essential issue and action. Don't try to look smart by confusing things or making a proposal that's so complicated nobody can understand it. This is also a good way to challenge yourself to focus on what's really important.

For more detailed discussion of this lesson, see pages 86-87.

Lesson 16: Don't be a commodity.

Commodities are products or services whose only (or primary) source of differentiation is price. If you're consulting for $100 an hour and the next guy is consulting for $80 an hour, you're both commodities. You're selling the same hours but at different prices. You'll be much better served if you focused on your unique contribution and high value. Then it won't always be a price issue. You'll deliver more value, and you'll make more money.

For more detailed discussion of this lesson, see pages 111-113.

Lesson 17: Price to value!

Everyone – even clients – would rather pay a premium price for service they perceive as superior than a discounted price for something they think is low value. Challenge yourself to deliver superior value and set your fees so that the client is paying a fair price and still getting a bargain. Consulting is a win-win deal.

For more detailed discussion of this lesson, see pages 93-97 and 113-114.

> *When his proposal was accepted, Greg wasted no time. He got to work and delivered everything he'd promised – and in record time to boot. Everyone on the client team was impressed. Clearly Greg had established his value and earned the right to bid on future projects.*

Lesson 18: Over-deliver against client expectations – and do it fast.

Clients always notice and remember how well a consultant performs. If it's their first time using an outside consultant, they may still not be sure it was the right thing to do (i.e., if it was worth the money). If they're frequent users of consulting services, they're comparing you to previous experiences. They can't help it; they're always evaluating your performance. And they decide early in the relationship how satisfied they are. Rarely do they wait until the project is finished to form lasting opinions. That's why a consultant has to make it a point to over-deliver against client expectations – and do it fast!

For more detialed discussion of this lesson, see pages 126-129.

Lesson 19: Establish your value/expertise as quickly as possible.

There's another reason you want to stake out your turf early: You're going to want and need the cooperation and support of the full client team in order to deliver the project. If team members genuinely respect what you bring to the party from the outset they'll help you. Otherwise they may "play it safe" and watch from the sidelines – or even withhold critical information to see if you're as good as you say you are.

For more detailed discussion of this lesson, see pages 44-46.

Lesson 20: Plan the future relationship as you deliver the initial project.

When you're doing your homework and gathering data for the initial project, you'll have the best opportunity of all to see what other problems a client has that you can address later. If you're alert to them, and make notes to yourself, you may find that you can either (a) add value to the current project by addressing an issue that is technically outside the scope of the project, or (b) lay the groundwork for a follow-on project that will prove to be of even higher value to the client. Don't view this as a way to increase your billing and extend the relationship; if you do, it may look like you're overstepping your bounds. Instead, think of it as a way to be helpful to the client; they'll almost certainly appreciate that attitude.

For more detailed discussion of this lesson, see pages 126-129 and 137.

Of course, there were those on the internal staff who felt threatened. After all, the new consultant had been able to solve a problem that had eluded them, and it was clear that his services would be needed on an ongoing basis. Greg was sensitive to their reaction and tried to befriend and support them as best he could. Nonetheless, he knew his first loyalty was to Number Two; Number Two was confident in giving Greg additional assignments and even introduced him to the Big Boss.

Lesson 21: Each deliverable should logically tie to the next project.

If you want to establish a long term consulting relationship, view each project in the context of the company's long-term objectives. Surely the client's smorgasbord of needs doesn't end when a project is delivered; they always have other, related needs that may follow directly from the project itself. Be sensitive to these broader needs. Not only will it give you ideas for a follow-on project, but it will show the client that you are not myopic in your view of their business – an important "extra" when they're assessing a consultant's value.

For more detailed discussion of this lesson, see pages 80-81 and 137.

Lesson 22: Remember who the client is and what success looks like for from his vantage point.

Very often in a consulting project, you get so wrapped up in the business or technical issues you're dealing with, and your own clever solutions to a client's problems, that you temporarily forget (a) what the original project objectives were, and (b) what other needs the individual client sponsor – the REAL client – had in mind when he or she hired you. Guard against this as best you can. If the client really wanted a confidante and personal career consultant, why risk the entire relationship by withholding those tacitly-agreed services?

For more detailed discussion of this lesson, see pages 42-43 and 99-105.

> *As time passed, Greg continued to deliver high value to his client, though the Big Boss never quite accepted him the way Number Two did. Then Greg got his big break: The Big Boss was reassigned and Number Two moved into the top spot. Greg was right where he wanted to be, making his unique contribution and being well rewarded for the high value he delivered.*

Lesson 23: Always place the client's best interests first.

This is an attitude thing more than anything else. If you keep the client's needs and best interests foremost in your thinking, you'll almost always find additional ways to be helpful and valuable, ensure that the project is on track toward meeting or exceeding the client's expectations, and solidify your own role in the relationship. How can that be wrong?

For more detailed discussion of this lesson, see pages 55 and 99-105.

Lesson 24: Be sure the client feels you're delivering value in excess of your cost.

It's not always easy to place a dollar value on a consultant's deliverable; sometime it's a "soft" benefit – like achieving better teamwork, or aligning everyone's interests toward the same goal, for example. Nonetheless, the client has obviously placed a value on your services, and it's at least as great as your fee – or you wouldn't have landed the project. Find a way early in the relationship to take your client's temperature and ensure that the project objectives and performance metrics haven't changed, and that the client is still comfortable with your contribution. It's better to learn about any problems early; at least you have an opportunity to adjust.

For more detailed discussion of this lesson, see pages 70 and 95-96.

For more detailed discussion of this lesson, see pages 70 and 95-96.

The story would end there were it not for growing resentment and hostility among the internal team. They were constantly being compared to the "brilliant consultant" and coming up second best. They had to find a way to remove him or they'd live in his shadow forever. And Greg refused to compromise his own standards of performance or shift his loyalties to win their acceptance. Besides, he'd gotten used to a pretty nice lifestyle and as much influence on important matters as an outsider could reasonably expect.

Lesson 25: Work hard to be accepted by the client team; discuss potential people problems with the client, and include people issues in the project proposal. You'll need to deal with them sooner or later, so better to be candid about them early.

Most projects – especially marketing or technically-oriented projects – don't explicitly include a definition of all the people issues associated with them. An astute consultant will identify these issues early in the relationship and develop a mini-plan to deal with them. After all, the key client individual has to live with his or her co-workers after the project ends, so anything you can do to make that person's life a little better will reflect well on both the project and the consultant.

For more detailed discussion of this lesson, see pages 57-58 and 71.

> *The inside team came up with a plan, arranging to give Greg an important assignment that no consultant could possibly deliver. When he failed, they used it as proof that "the magic was gone" and Greg was back on the street, out of work once again. From a career standpoint, he was finished. No client would hire the high-profile consultant who lost his touch and failed.*

Lesson 26: Never accept an assignment that you don't think you can master. Consulting is a "zero tolerance" business.

I don't know of a single instance where a consultant was able to fully recover after botching a major project and disappointing the client. In that sense, consulting is a very unforgiving business. The old saying about being "only as good as your last project" is never more true than it is in consulting. Any consultant who accepts an assignment that he's not sure he can master is sealing his own fate. A client paying big fees does not expect the consultant to just be learning the skills he's supposed to have already.

For more detailed discussion of this lesson, see pages 99-100 and 128.

Appendices

Appendix A

The Evil Monk

The life and times of
Grigori Yefimovich Rasputin

By Arturo Beéche

No other figure in Russian history has received the amount of vilification and contempt heaped upon Grigori Rasputin. The self-styled monk, who received virtually no education in the intricacies of the Russian Orthodox faith, came from the rural areas of Russia and achieved great recognition as a "staretz," or holy man in the highest circles of St. Petersburg society. From rags to social prominence, the life of Grigori Rasputin is intertwined with many of the events leading to the eventual overthrow of the Russian imperial system, the dethronement of the House of Romanov, and the assassination of the Imperial Family.

Grigori Yefimovich Rasputin came from solid peasant stock. He was born on January 10, 1869, in Prokovskoe, a small village in Siberia on the banks of the Tura River. As a young lad, Rasputin shocked his village by constantly finding ways to get into trouble with the authorities. Drunkenness, stealing, and womanizing were activities particularly enjoyed by the dissolute young man. Rasputin in fact was developing into a rake, a man with a debauched, and endless, sexual appetite.It was while on one of his escapades that Rasputin was first impacted by the mystical powers of the Russian Orthodox religion. At Verkhoturye Monastery Rasputin was fascinated by a renegade sect within the Orthodox faith, the Skopsty. Followers of the Skopsty firmly believed that the only way to reach God was through sinful actions. Once the sin was committed and confessed, the penitent could achieve forgiveness. In reality, what the Skopsty upheld was to "sin to drive out sin." Rasputin, one of the biggest sinners of the province, was suddenly struck by the potential held by this theory. It was soon thereafter that the debauched, lecherous peasant adopted the robes of a monk, developed his own self-gratifying doctrines, traveled the country as a "staretz," and sinned to his heart's content.

By the time he reached his early thirties, Rasputin had traveled to the Holy Land and back. It was while in Kazan that the mysterious traveling monk made an impression among the local clergy. It was with the recommendations of these fooled priests that Rasputin headed to St. Petersburg for his first visit. While in the Russian capital, Rasputin's presence attracted the attention of many of the country's leading religious leaders. The staretz' traveling tales, as well as the stories he told about his religious revival, seemed to capture the attention of the higher clergy of the Russian empire. The year was 1902.

The Tsar's death seemed imminent as his once strong body caved under the strain of his sickness. No one would have thought that Tsar Alexander III, a giant by most accounts, would be dead before his fiftieth year. And no one was more terrified by the events unfolding at the Imperial compound at Livadia, in the Crimea, as the young heir, Tsarevich Nicholas Alexandrovich. At the time of his father's death in late 1894, Nicholas was an inexperienced youth wholly unprepared for the great task destiny had placed on his shoulders. Nicholas himself was terribly aware of this and upon his father's death, the new Tsar consoled himself by asking God to give him the guidance and strength to carry out the impossible burdens of ruling the complex and vastly complicated Russian empire.

Nicholas II was barely twenty-six years old at the time of his accession. During his son's golden youth, Alexander III did not

Appendix A: The Evil Monk

allow his son Nicholas much participation in affairs of government. It is likely that Alexander III feared that his eldest son was not intellectually capable of handling the inheritance that was rightfully his. Therefore, the father kept postponing the son's introduction in to the daily running of Russia. Not one person, most of all Alexander III, ever imagined that this young and inexperienced Romanov would ascend the throne as early in life as he did.

Nicholas II's mother, the Empress Maria-Feodorovna, was largely responsible for continuing her son's adolescence into his twenties. The Empress, a doting mother at best, refused to let her children grow. This behavior would have dire consequences in the future, particularly as the responsibilities of royal life entered the lives of her children. Not only would Nicholas marry a princess whom Maria-Feodorovna and Alexander III did not like, but also her other surviving son, the Grand Duke Michael Alexandrovich married a twice-divorced commoner. The misfortune of her children was also extended to the imperial couple's youngest daughter, the Grand Duchess Olga Alexandrovna, who was forced to marry Duke Peter of Oldenburg, a minor German prince whose family had settled in Russia and who was notoriously known as one of the most scandalous members of St. Petersburg society.

Alexander and Maria-Feodorovna's opposition to Nicholas' marriage caused the dying Tsar much distress. Years before, Nicholas had made the acquaintance of Princess Alix of Hesse and by Rhine who was the youngest sister of Grand Duchess Elisabeth Feodorovna, wife of Nicholas' uncle Grand Duke Serge Alexandrovich. Alix was also the granddaughter of Prince Charles of Hesse and by Rhine, who in turn was a brother of Empress Maria Alexandrovna, mother of Tsar Alexander III. Thus, Nicholas and Alix were third cousins. More importantly, at least from a dynastic standpoint, Princess Alix was one of the favorite granddaughters of Queen Victoria of Great Britain. Still, Alexander and

Maria-Feodorovna saw Alix as a very poor choice for a bride and opposed Nicholas' intentions to marry his melancholic German love.

The threat of Nicholas remaining unmarried and thus risking the imperial succession ultimately forced Alexander and Maria-Feodorovna to consent to their son's marriage. At Coburg, during the marriage of Grand Duke Ernst-Ludwig of Hesse and by Rhine, Alix's brother, to Princess Victoria Melita of Saxe-Coburg-Gotha, Nicholas finally obtained Alix's consent to his marriage proposal. The developing relationship between Nicholas and Alix overshadow the wedding celebrations of Victoria Melita and Ernst-Ludwig, an affront that the Coburg bride would never forget.

Alexander III died at the age of forty-nine on October 20, 1894. He was at the imperial palace in Livadia, the Crimea, and was surrounded by his afflicted family. Nicholas and Alix, who soon after the Tsar's death joined the Russian Orthodox church as Alexandra Feodorovna, were married within a week of Alexander's death. The marriage took place in the midst of the overwhelming mourning that had engulfed the lives of all the members of the imperial family.

There is very little question that Nicholas and Alexandra loved each other intensely, even to the point of isolating themselves from the rest of their family and the country as a whole. They were happiest when away from society and surrounded by the seclusion of their official residence at the Alexander Palace in Tsarskoe Selo. Within a year of their hasty wedding, the couple became parents to a plump little girl, the Grand Duchess Olga Nicholaievna. Three more daughters were to follow: Tatiana Nicholaievna born in 1897, Maria Nicholaievna born in 1899 and Anastasia Nicholaievna born in 1901. Loving as they were as parents, Nicholas and Alexandra were deeply concerned at their inability to provide an heir to the imperial throne. After the birth of their fourth daughter, the couple desperately sought all sorts of help to insure that the next child would be a boy. The desire for Alexandra to produce a boy developed into a fixation. Mystics, faith healers and staretz found themselves in great demand at the Alexander Palace. Most of these people were of doubtful reputation but since they were sponsored by the Grand Duchesses Milita and Anastasia, daughters of King Nicholas of Montenegro and married to two of Nicholas' cousins, Nicholas and Alexandra received them with intense hopes that the arrival of a son would thus be guaranteed.

By late 1903 Alexandra found herself pregnant again. Intense praying and mysticism accompanied her throughout the pregnancy, and finally on July 30, 1904, a little boy was born. Nicholas and Alexandra called him Alexis in memory of the second Romanov tsar. The heir became the center of the family's attention as a delighted imperial couple reveled in the joy of finally having an heir they could call their own. Despite the couple's delight, within months of Alexis' birth a dark cloud settled over the imperial nursery. Alexis's body, once injured, would not stop bleeding. The Tsarevich was another victim of the dreaded disease inherited from his great-grandmother Queen Victoria, Hemophilia. Nicholas accepted this new trial with stoic fatalism, and Alexandra blamed herself for her son's affliction. The Tsar's brother-in-law, Grand Duke Alexander Michaelovich, once said that Alexandra "refused to surrender to fate ... she talked incessantly of the ignorance of the physicians. She professed an open preference for medicine men. She turned toward religion ... but her prayers were tainted with a certain hysteria. The stage was set for the appearance of a miracle worker."

At the time of Alexis' birth several of Queen Victoria's descendants were sufferers of the disease. Victoria's granddaughter, Princess Irene of Hesse and by Rhine, wife of Prince Henry of Prussia, had two hemophiliac sons. Victoria's youngest son, Prince Leopold, Duke of Albany, had died as a result of a bleeding. Some of the Queen's other granddaughters, Princess Victoria of

Battenberg and Princess Alice of Albany, would pass the disease to their children. Alexandra Feodorovna and her sister Irene had lost a brother to the disease as well. It seemed to many that the price for marrying into Victoria's powerful family was running the risk of bringing hemophilia into the royal palaces of Europe.

The first decade of Alexandra's life in Russia were marred by the continued absence of a male heir. The second decade of her life among the Romanovs was devastated by the disease that martyred her only son. When hemophilia first manifested itself in Alexis, Nicholas wrote in his diary that "it was a dreadful thing to have to live through such anxiety." By the time Alexis was one year old, he again was afflicted by a more serious bleeding episode. The imperial couple's anxiety was accentuated by doctors who told them they "had to realize that the heir apparent will never be cured of this disease. The attacks of hemophilia will recur now and then ..."

In the midst of this tragedy within the imperial family, Rasputin returned to St. Petersburg after a two-year hiatus. Initially, Rasputin moved prudently in the Russian capital's aristocratic circles. He tried, unsuccessfully, to restrain his debauched, womanizing ways, yet temptation was overwhelming. Within months, Rasputin, the saintly sinner, had achieved recognition and a small following in St. Petersburg. Besides gaining the friendship of Grand Duchess Militza and Anastasia, Rasputin also gained the trust of Anna Vyrubova, Empress Alexandra's trusted companion. It was under the recommendation of the Grand Duchesses and Anna Vyrubova that Rasputin was summoned to appear before Alexandra.

Rasputin managed to bring calm and hope into the lives of Nicholas and Alexandra. Most importantly, the staretz was capable of putting a stop to the Alexis' bleedings. Many people have tried to explain the nature of Rasputin's power over the poor little boy. Some have claimed that Rasputin did indeed have holy powers. Others believe that Rasputin was able to hypnotize Alexis and therefore cause the bleedings to stop. However Rasputin managed to stop Alexis' suffering, the truth of the matter was that he gained Nicholas and Alexandra's undivided support.

As the monk's star rose in St. Petersburg, so did the number of his enemies. Many of the Orthodox clergymen who had initially supported Rasputin became skeptical about his relationship with the imperial couple. St. Petersburg society also failed to understand the bonds that brought Rasputin into such close proximity to the throne. Nicholas and Alexandra had refused to inform their subjects about Alexis' sickness, thus it baffled many to see the imperial couple in dealings with such a lecherous rake as Rasputin. Soon enough, the rumor mills of St. Petersburg accused Alexandra of being romantically, and even sexually involved with the monk. More pernicious gossips even extended the rumors to include the couple's four daughters who supposedly had become Rasputin's sex toys. It is inconceivable that someone as upright and unbending as Alexandra would have ever considered such vile behavior. Yet it is also inconceivable that the rumors were allowed to continue while the reputation of the imperial couple fell to pieces. No one was more responsible for the growing rumors than Rasputin himself. During his many drunken parties, the monk would boast of his exploits with the Empress and her daughters, even going as far as proclaiming that the Tsar was at his fingertips.

Nicholas's secret police quickly informed the Tsar of these rumors. A penitent Rasputin was summoned to appear before the infuriated Tsar, but Alexandra defended the staretz. Nicholas punished Rasputin by sending him back to the provinces, but no sooner had Rasputin left when another bleeding crisis almost killed Alexis. Rasputin's influence over the boy guaranteed the monk's return to St. Petersburg. His position within the imperial circle was never again challenged. Alexandra grew completely dependent on the man, who not only became her son's faith healer, but also the

Empress' confidant. The evil monk's presence among the Tsar and his family would further alienate them from the capital and all those circles that had traditionally been the mainstay of tsarism. Nicholas and Alexandra were doomed from that point on.

On June 28, 1914, while the Russian Imperial Yacht Standart sailed along the Baltic coastline, the Archduke Franz-Ferdinand of Habsburg and his wife were assassinated in Sarajevo. Within weeks of this vile act of regicide all of Europe was in a flurry of prewar preparations. The great moment to define European mastery had arrived. The arrival of war surprised practically everyone. At the time of Franz-Ferdinand's assassination no one in Europe believed the act would lead to war between the great empires of the time. The Tsar continued on his cruise, the Kaiser sailed along the Norwegian coast, and the French president prepared his entourage for a state visit to St. Petersburg. All along the continent European royalty visited their royal cousins in countries that were about to declare war on each other.

When Vienna decided to declare war on Serbia, using the involvement of Serbian government officials in the assassination of Franz-Ferdinand as an excuse, Russia could not stand idly by. On one opportunity when Austria had annexed Bosnia-Herzegovina in 1908, Nicholas had been unable to come to the rescue of his fellow Slavs. On this new affront to Slavdom, the Tsar took a stand and geared his country for war against Austria-Hungary. Germany being Austria's ally, a move against Vienna would mean that St. Petersburg would also have to fight Berlin. Paris and London watched hopelessly as the crowned heads of Europe forgot their family ties and recent summer visits to take up the dangerous flag of nationalism. A state of war between the Russia and Germany and Austria was declared by the first week of August.

However bellicose the Russians felt, the country was completely unprepared to fight against formidable enemies such as

Appendix A: The Evil Monk

Germany and Austria. The Russian supply lines were inefficient, there were not enough rifles for as many soldiers as Russia had, new recruits were often sent to the front without even the proper clothing and not enough ammunition. Corruption within the Russian weapons' supply system was rampant and several army officers made vast fortunes at the expense of the lives of hundreds of thousands of Russian victims. The leadership of the Russian military forces was given to the Grand Duke Nicholas Nicholaievich, a cousin of the Tsar and the husband of Grand Duchess Anastasia, the woman responsible for sponsoring Rasputin. Grand Duke Nicholas desperately tried to reverse the initial Russian losses, but given the resources he had this was a Herculean task. Consequently, the country's military effort continued to suffer dismal setbacks. Rasputin himself sent a note to the Grand Duke Nicholas offering to visit his headquarters to bless the troops, but the Grand Duke Nicholas, one of Rasputin's most vehement opponents, replied "Yes, do come. I'll hang you."

The Grand Duke Nicholas' reactions towards Rasputin exemplified the high level of frustration felt by the Romanov family concerning the relationship of Nicholas and Alexandra and the hated monk. As the war progressed, the Russian government simply collapsed under the weight of the enormous efforts demanded by the armies and the obtuse leadership provided by Tsar Nicholas II. It certainly did not help matters when it was discovered that Nicholas was also relying on Alexandra for the day-to-day handling of governmental affairs. And since Alexandra and Rasputin were in close contact, many believed that indeed it was Rasputin who had become the true lord of All the Russias. Nicholas's family, even his mother, desperately tried to have the monk removed from the imperial couple's proximity. The Romanovs, never really fond of Alexandra, constantly approached the Tsar and demanded that Rasputin be sent away. Nicholas, blinded by his love for Alexandra and fearful of risking Alexis' life, rudely dismissed his family's entreaties. Rasputin's influence continued and the Imperial Family's image continued to be tainted with opprobrium and scandal emanating from the actions of the evil monk.

Nicholas II's biggest mistake was dismissing Grand Duke Nicholas Nicholaievich in 1915 and assuming command of the Russian armies. Inefficient as a ruler, mainly due to his lack of preparation for the office, Nicholas II was a dismal military commander as well. Encouraged by his wife, who had a deep dislike for the Grand Duke Nicholas, the Tsar convinced himself that his place was among his troops. Consequently, Nicholas left Petrograd, as the capital was then called to avoid using a German sounding name, and headed for military headquarters. In his place, and to act in his stead, Nicholas II left none other than his beloved Alexandra. The Empress, regardless of her later martyrdom and previous suffering, was simply the most incompetent choice available to Nicholas. If Rasputin's influence with Alexandra was checked by Nicholas prior to his departure, now that Tsar was away from Petrograd Rasputin became the Empress' chief counsel. The Russian imperial government basically disintegrated as ministers were fired and quickly replaced by many of Rasputin's supporters. Accountability for the growing corruption within the government simply disappeared as the country headed towards utter chaos and ruin. Regardless of the martyrdom suffered by Nicholas, Alexandra and their children, one cannot ignore the damaging role played in the demise of the Romanovs by Alexandra. Incapable of ruling, married to a husband who would have been happiest as a country squire instead of a Tsar of All the Russias, Alexandra's attempt at single-handedly governing Russia was doomed to failure. Isolated from Russia's realities, blinded in her devotion to Rasputin, fearful for her son's survival, Alexandra was in no position to effectively fill the absence left by Nicholas' decision to join his armies. Indeed,

Appendix A: The Evil Monk

both Nicholas and Alexandra are greatly, if not solely, responsible for the ignominious end the Romanov dynasty faced in 1917-18.

Frustrated by their inability to break down the walls built by Nicholas and Alexandra, some members of the Romanov family took events into their own hands. How many of the Romanovs were involved in the actual plotting to assassinate Rasputin will never be known for certain. What is widely accepted is that the Tsar's cousin, Grand Duke Dimitri Pavlovich and Prince Felix Youssoupov, husband of Nicholas II's niece Princess Irina Alexandrovna of Russia, were among the leaders of the plot to strike against Rasputin. The monk, always frustrated by the Romanov's opposition to his role in Russia, was invited by Youssoupov to attend an evening gathering at his vast Petrograd palace. Felix promised Rasputin that his wife Irina would be there to greet him. The monk fell in the trap and willingly arrived at the Youssoupov palace in the evening of December 16, 1916. He did not survive the evening.

During the fateful last evening of Rasputin's life, the conspirators drugged, poisoned, beat and shot him. Yet the staretz survived all these and actually died by drowning when his body, wrapped in a carpet was thrown into the Moika Canal on the Neva River.

By the morrow Prince Felix Youssoupov was under questioning by the Petrograd police. So messy had been the assassins that proof of their deed was found all over the Youssoupov palace. Within hours of the report concerning Rasputin's disappearance, the Petrograd police by orders of Alexandra, forbid the conspirators from leaving the Russian capital. As soon as he received news of events in Petrograd Nicholas boarded his train and hurriedly returned to the capital. Rasputin's corpse was discovered under the ice of the Neva on December 19. The fury and outrage expressed by Nicholas and Alexandra knew no bounds as they sought to punish all of the conspirators. At the same time, news of Rasputin's death caused widespread eruptions of rapture in Petrograd. Dimitri and Felix were heralded as heroes and many believed that the "alleged" German influence represented by Alexandra was going to stop.

While the Petrograd elite enjoyed their supposed liberation from Rasputin's clutches, the vast majority of the Russian population saw the events in a completely different light. For 80% of the Russian population Rasputin was a "man of the people." He was their hope that the imperial couple would never forget the plight of the peasantry. His assassination at the hands of aristocrats, and even members of the imperial family, robbed the upper classes of much support among the inhabitants of their estates.

In the end, Nicholas sent his two wayward relatives into exile. Ironically enough, it was this punishment what allowed Dimitri and Felix to avoid falling in the hands of Bolsheviks during the revolution. Within three months of Rasputin's death, Nicholas lost his throne, the imperial family was imprisoned and many of the Romanov cousins arrested. In the end almost twenty members of the Romanov family were massacred by Bolshevik firing squads. No other epitaph to Rasputin's death better exemplifies the repercussions of the monk's death than that written by Grand Duchess Maria Pavlova, sister, in her Memoirs: "His death came too late to change the course of events. His dreadful name had become too thoroughly a symbol of disaster. The daring of those who killed him to save their country was miscalculated. All of the participants in the plot, with the exception of Prince Youssoupov later understood that in raising their hands to preserve the old regime they struck it, in reality, its final blow."

* * * * *

This synopsis of Rasputin's life is reprinted with permission from an article by Arturo Beeche. Arturo is Publisher and Editor of The European

Appendix A: The Evil Monk

Royal History Journal, *and he maintains a website for devotees at* www.eurohistory.com. *His article is based on information from Greg King's* "The Man Who Killed Rasputin," *Alex de Yonge's* "Rasputin," *Robert K. Massie's* "Nicholas and Alexandra," *and Prince Felix Youssoupov's* "Lost Splendour."

Appendix B

A Sample Project Proposal

Ms. Jane Doe, President
ABC Assessment Corporation
One Fictitious Drive
Smallville, New Hampshire

Dear Jane:

Subject: **Strategic Plan to Achieve Corporate Objectives**

Per your request, this provides our proposal to create a strategic plan
for ABC Assessment Corporation that will enable the company to:

(a) dramatically expand awareness of and favorable
    disposition toward the ABC brand franchise
    among senior HR and general management
    executives in the United States;

(b) ensure that the scope and quality of services
    delivered are consistent with the expectations and
    requirements of ABC's customer base; and

(c) generate profitable new business that will allow
    ABC to achieve its short- and intermediate-tem
    goals for revenue and profitability.

The project itself would begin immediately upon acceptance of this
proposal and span a period of approximately 7-9 months. At the end
of the project, we would present findings, conclusions, indicated
actions, and specific recommendations in a half-day meeting with the
ABC Executive Committee, and provide a comprehensive and detailed
written report for later reference.

Rasputin For Hire

Background

ABC Assessment Corporation is a leading firm in the development of individual and team performance measurement, with a portfolio of proprietary assessment instruments that have been successfully utilized in a number of major corporations throughout the world. Common applications include pre-employment evaluation, enhancing team effectiveness, leadership skills training, time management, merging disparate corporate cultures, and job stress reduction.

The Company sells and distributes its products and related services through a network of independent Certified Practitioners who are trained in the appropriate use of all ABC instruments and applications, and who have agreed to maintain a set of procedures and performance standards as part of their certification process with the Company. Revenues are shared between the practitioners and ABC Assessment Corporation according to a published schedule.

The practitioners who actually implement ABC programs are encouraged to work with the Company to develop additional uses for the basic instruments and their underlying technology, and many applications that began as "one-off" solutions to specific problems have eventually become important elements in a standardized offering.

While the Company enjoys broad awareness and support worldwide, the United States remains both the largest market for ABC products and services (approximately 75% last year) and the market thought to hold the greatest potential for short-term growth.

ABC Assessment's Executive Committee has made a commitment to "take the business to the next level" and established an ambitious 5-year growth objective. We have been asked to develop a strategic plan that will enable ABC to achieve that objective and payout any front-loaded investment by the end of the 5-year period.

Appendix B: A Sample Project Proposal

Summary of Proposal

Given your agreement to this proposal, we will develop a comprehensive strategic plan that will form the foundation for detailed marketing plans and programs keyed to the achievement of ABC's growth objectives over the next 5 years.

We will consider opportunities within the current customer base, prime targets for short-term growth, and attractive longer-term approaches that require more lead time. We will also consider the investment required to achieve the target growth goals, implications for the infrastructure (i.e., the Certified Practitioner approach, training, recruiting, etc.), and the full spectrum of marketing mix issues.

In all of these areas, we will be sensitive to accurately identifying legitimate customer needs, objectively assessing the appropriateness of ABC's offering to address those needs, and defining the business model/structure and marketing approach that will best allow ABC to deliver full value to its Certified Practitioners and clients on a competitive basis while generating a fair profit for the Company.

The ultimate deliverable for this effort will be a full-blown strategic plan, presented to ABC's Executive Committee and supported by detailed rationale, budget estimates, assessment of the barriers/risks, and a detailed path forward recommendation. We will, of course, be available to discuss the proposed plan in detail and to answer any questions that might arise. Documentation in the form of report books will be provided for future reference.

The project itself will span a period of 7-9 months. We will begin with an initial start-up meeting; continue with interviews of key headquarters and field personnel, development of positioning and overall strategic options, and consideration of all marketing mix elements; and end with a formal presentation of findings, conclusions, indicated action, and specific path forward recommendations.

Work Plan

We see five distinct phases in this project, largely conducted and completed in sequence:

> **Phase I:** **Situation Analysis** – 10-12 weeks
> **Phase II:** **Positioning** – 6-8 weeks
> **Phase III:** **Overall Strategy Development** – 6-8 weeks
> **Phase IV:** **Marketing Mix Implications** – 4-6 weeks
> **Phase V:** **Presentation** – 3-4 weeks

When possible, we will dovetail/overlap the various work plan elements, but do not believe it is reasonable to expect that the total timing can be compressed more than a few weeks beyond the sum of the estimates shown.

Phase I: Situation Analysis

The situation analysis provides the foundation for the project and requires a thorough and structured plan for understanding the marketplace. We will begin the process with a start-up meeting at which the work plan for the project will be discussed and refined, and key process decision points are identified.

We would then interview: key managers at ABC headquarters, including all members of the Executive Committee; four or five selected Certified Practitioners in the field (at least two of whom are "stars" and at least one who is struggling); five or six current or recent ABC clients; and – if possible – one or two prospective clients who have not yet made a decision/commitment.

Prior to interviews in the field, we will prepare by reviewing a sampling of reports from recent projects, appropriate articles in trade journals, brochures, proposals, and whatever competitive information we can obtain.

Appendix B: A Sample Project Proposal

To ensure that we get complete, reliable, and candid input, we would utilize the Semi-Structured Interview format we pioneered, with a discussion guide developed specifically for ABC. In the 18 years we have been utilizing this approach, it has proven to be highly effective at getting people to share information, opinions, and perspectives in a non-threatening way. A full explanation of the technique is shown in the attached exhibit.

As a side note we would offer that it has been our experience that interviewing outside experts (e.g., Certified Practitioners, clients, and prospective clients) invariably strengthens their loyalty to the client company. Most people are flattered to be included in a research study and frequently share useful insights with the "outsider" that might never be discussed with company personnel.

Finally, we would want to review/discuss marketing initiatives that ABC has considered or tried in the past, to understand how well they worked, what problems there were (if any), and how the various constituencies responded.

With this information in hand, we would summarize and analyze our findings and use them as a basis for planning the path forward.

The timing for the situation analysis is mostly a function of scheduling and availability for interview subjects. While we would like to complete it in a month or two, it has been our experience – especially with vacations, holiday schedules, etc. – that 10-12 weeks is more realistic.

Phase II: Positioning

Once the situation analysis is complete, we would begin an interactive dialogue with the ABC marketing team and advertising agency to understand the Company's communication history and desired positioning, and to compare/contrast those to what we learn in the interviews. The objective of this process would be to create and agree on a Positioning Statement that can be used going forward.

We would then plan to lead a team of 4-6 ABC managers in a day-long workshop, the output of which would be an initial draft of the Positioning Statement going forward. We would challenge and perhaps suggest refinements to the draft over a period of 2-3 weeks before settling on a working positioning platform. Of course, it could still be refined further based on new input or perspective, but we would hope to be very close to a final version at that point.

This process will need to span a period of approximately 6-8 weeks to allow time for reflection, gestation, and revision. This is a critically important step in the total process, and we are concerned that it could run the risk of being done poorly if it is rushed. Very often the best positioning ideas crop up just after end of the formal interaction, and we would not want to miss a useful and valuable creative element because we were overly focused on the timetable.

Phase III: Overall Strategy Development

With the situation analysis and a working positioning platform in hand, we would consider the various elements of an overall strategy and develop the key components of a strategic marketing plan.

In this phase of the project we would specifically address the issue of where new business would come from – expanding within current clients, developing new applications using the same basic technology, aggressively soliciting new "low-hanging-fruit" clients, adding more Certified Practitioners, re-training current Certified Practitioners, restructuring the delivery process, adding field management, etc. We would also consider implications of each option on the Company infrastructure and support elements.

One area we would examine carefully in this context is the sales-versus-consultant role of each Certified Practitioner. For the most part, the Certified Practitioners are technically expert in the administration and delivery of ABC Assessment's products and services; they are not trained sales professionals or consultants. We would need to determine how we can either improve their selling and consulting skills or separate the functions and have a separate team of experts who only sell and manage client relationships. We see this as a critical issue, given the need to dramatically expand the revenue base. Of course, we would consider the organizational and cost implications of the various options before making a recommendation.

This phase of the project should take about 6-8 weeks and will involve some limited interaction with the ABC management team, though it will be mostly an independent work plan element for us.

Phase IV: Marketing Mix Implications

Because the Positioning Platform (from Phase II) and the Overall Strategy (from Phase III) will be in place at this point, we will be in a position to develop a set of strategies that encompass all the other elements of the marketing mix. Then in an iterative fashion, we can modify and adjust all plan elements to ensure that the total plan is internally consistent and likely to deliver the desired outcome.

To do this, we will specifically develop initial approaches in each of the following marketing areas:

Product/offering	Pricing	Sales/Distribution
Packaging	Promotion	Advertising
Publicity	Service	

We will ensure that the strategies in each area are supportive of the Positioning and consistent with the Overall Strategy, and that they are mutually supportive/consistent as well. We will create a rough budget for each area to (a) indicate its relative importance within the mix, and (b) allow us to project the likely total cost of the marketing initiative.

This effort will require approximately 4-6 weeks, as we will want to carefully assess the likely return on investment for each of the marketing mix elements as well as the total plan.

Phase V: Presentation

When all of the planning elements (from Phases I-IV) are completed, we will organize and prepare a document and slide presentation to explain and share the complete methodology, findings, conclusions, indicated actions, and our recommended path forward. We will present this at a meeting of the ABC Executive Committee that will probably require 3-4 hours, including ample time for questions and discussion of key issues. Then we will provide all attendees with a book containing the presentation materials and detailed support documents.

We would recommend that a follow-up meeting be scheduled a week or two after the presentation so that we can reconvene to gain full buy-in and commitment to the plan, incorporate any after-thoughts or new ideas, and provide a kind of closure for the management team. The project report book, and a group review of key exhibits in it, can be the focal point for preparing for the follow-up meeting. (We have seen this approach work very effectively many times.)

We would want approximately a month to prepare for the presentation and organize the project report books. While we will be preparing most of the material as we proceed through the project, we've found that the presentation format and organization are often more complicated than they initially appear, and the extra few weeks will be well worth the wait in terms of clearly communicating the strategic plan elements and their likely impact on the business.

Staffing

This project would be managed and delivered by me, Michael A. Goodman, and a small team from Dialogue. We are fully qualified for this based on several factors:

1. We all have strong credentials and several years' experience in developing marketing strategy and business planning, including projects very much like the one we are proposing for ABC

Appendix B: A Sample Project Proposal

Assessment Corporation. We pioneered the development of the Semi-Structured Interview format and have used it effectively in dozens of situations like this one. And we have developed marketing and business plans for other clients that have successfully achieved very ambitious growth objectives – just like ABC's.

2. We have seen the ABC Assessment approach work at a shared client (XYZ Corporation) and genuinely believe it is the most effective instrument/technology of its kind. Based on that experience, we are and have been "product believers" who are eager to help spread the word and position the Company to other client companies who can benefit from the ABC offering.

3. We have developed and delivered numerous workshops on Positioning and Branding, and have high confidence that we can deliver a strong and effective Positioning Platform for ABC. As we have discussed, this is perhaps the single most important element in the project as it provides the foundation for all the other elements of the marketing mix and the strategic plan that will ultimately be implemented.

4. We have recently been through the ABC certification process, so we not only have the kind of in-depth understanding of the subject that you would expect from a trained practitioner, but also some initial familiarity with the kinds of individuals who typically seek certification (i.e., one of the key constituencies in this project).

5. We have the time, interest, and enthusiasm for this project and would welcome the opportunity to make a contribution to your business.

Timing and Fee

As discussed above, the project will span a period of approximately 7-9 months – starting in June and running through early next year. We would expect to actually schedule the final presentation shortly before year-end – as we move into Phase IV and have a pretty good idea of how the timing is unfolding.

The fee for this project will be $275,000, plus reimbursement for required and approved travel expenses. We would bill the project in four installments: 25% in advance (i.e., upon acceptance of this proposal); 25% when Phase I is completed; 25% as Phase III is completed; and the balance on completion and delivery of the final presentation and report. Travel expenses would be billed monthly as incurred.

You will notice that the fee is somewhat lower than most projects of this kind (typically in the $300-350,000 range). Please be assured that we are not sacrificing quality, staffing, speed or intensity of effort. The reason for the lower-than-normal fee is that we already have considerable familiarity with ABC Assessment Corporation, its management, core products, and underlying technology. Our up-front research will therefore be much easier and faster than most, and we are reflecting the efficiency we expect to realize as a result.

At this level, the financial return to ABC Assessment should be quite rapid and significant. Gross profit from incremental business is in excess of 65% of sales, and achieving the Company's growth goal would generate far more in profit (than the project fee) in just the first twelve months after implementation. Incremental gross profit after that would fall directly to the bottom line and/or be available for further reinvestment.

Next Steps

We are prepared to devote the time and effort necessary for this project starting in June. All we need is your approval to proceed; a phone call or e-mail message will suffice. Immediately thereafter, we would set up the initial meeting to review work plan elements and begin to schedule appropriate interviews.

At your convenience, we should probably have a signed project agreement in place, with copies for each of us. This proposal can serve as that document. Simply sign and return one copy for our files and retain the other for yours.

* * * * *

We're very enthusiastic about this project, Jane, and know we can deliver a strategic plan that will meet your objectives, be perceived as high-value by the entire Management Committee, and ultimately put ABC Assessment Corporation exactly where you want it.

Thanks in advance for your support and cooperation.

Yours truly,

Michael A. Goodman

ACCEPTED:

_____   _____
Jane Doe, President   Date
ABC Assessment Corporation

Appendix C

Positioning Workshop Notes

Positioning is the image people have in their minds of your company or brand.

Positioning is more than what you tell them or what they observe. It includes what things others may have said or implied, the message(s) they actually received, and how they compare and contrast you with your direct and indirect competitors.

You can control what you tell people about your intended positioning, but you can't control what they perceive or think about you, or what others tell them about you. Perception is reality, and what your target audience PERCEIVES is your positioning.

What this means is that your actions will speak louder than your words when it comes to establishing a strong positioning.

If you already have an established product or company, you have a positioning – whether you intended it or not. Your customers and potential customers have an image, or impression, of your company/brand in their heads. Either they got it from your actions and what you've told them, or your competitors have positioned you (intentionally or otherwise).

If you have a brand new company or brand, you have the opportunity to establish the positioning you want with a clean slate.

The Positioning Statement

A good place to start the positioning process is with a carefully worded (and carefully considered) Positioning Statement. The actual writing process is important, but not nearly as important as the considerations and thinking process that precede it.

Start with a clear description of your primary target audience. If there are multiple audiences, be sure to identify each of them and determine which is really most important. You'll need to understand what makes your target audience tick before you can begin the positioning process. After all, positioning is what THEY think, not what you think. (And you really don't want multiple positioning statements; that will only confuse everyone.)

After clear identification of the primary target audience, a good Positioning Statement has two essential elements: (1) the key benefit promise, and (2) the "reason-why," or basis on which your target audience should believe the promise.

The **key benefit promise** is a clear and simple exposition of the most important benefit your company (or brand) will deliver. The **reason-why** is the rationale that will help the target audience accept the promise; it's an explanation that lends credibility.

There are a number of guidelines for a good Positioning Statement:

√ It should be focused, single-minded, and memorable.
√ It should be benefit-oriented.
√ It must be true ... not exaggerated, not a wish-list.
√ It should be believable ... not challenge credibility.

188

√ It should be unique and competitive.
√ It must be substantive, relevant, and important to the target audience.
√ It should capture and reflect the most important source of competitive advantage.

The actual wording is almost as important as the thinking. Don't make the mistake of assuming "everyone will understand." Be precise.

And don't make the mistake of confusing the Positioning Statement with a slogan or catch-phrase. The Positioning Statement is for internal use only and needs to be as substantive, technically precise, and accurate as it can be. Once it has been determined there will be time to develop public expressions and slogans.

Test for the "Positioning Magic-tives" – "first," "best," and "only." If the Positioning Statement doesn't communicate one or more of those, keep trying.

There are three possible levels of benefit: (1) direct benefit, (2) end benefit, and (3) end-end benefit. Whenever possible, seek to deliver and communicate the end or end-end benefit. It's more difficult, but it's also much more powerful and well worth the extra time and effort.

Using the Positioning Statement

When everyone is in agreement with the Positioning Statement it will serve as the foundation for all the other elements of the traditional marketing mix, and all the components of the marketing plan will reinforce the Positioning:

Product/Offering	Pricing
Promotion	Packaging
Sales/Distribution	Publicity
Advertising	

Be sure you consider how the Positioning Statement will affect each of these marketing mix elements, and be prepared to adjust it if/as you find opportunities to strengthen the positioning platform. The fine-tuning is an iterative process.

One final observation: Perhaps the most important element in creating an effective Positioning platform is prior experience. If you have created positioning platforms and statements before, you're more likely to do a better job, faster and easier, than if you're going through the process for the first time. And, given the importance of Positioning, it is worth a lot to have the most effective positioning from the outset. After all, you don't want to have to change a positioning after you've spent a lot of time, money, and energy establishing it. That's why most marketers call in outside expertise when they are faced with positioning a new product or rethinking one for an existing company or product/service.

Appendix D

The Institute of Management Consultants

Mission

To promote excellence and ethics in management consulting through certification, education, and professional resources

Code of Ethics

All members pledge in writing to abide by the Institute's Code of Ethics. Their adherence to the Code signifies voluntary assumption of self-discipline above and beyond the requirements of law.

Key provisions of the Code specify:

Clients

- Members will serve their clients with integrity, competence, and objectivity, using a professional approach at all times, and placing the best interests of the client above all others.

- Members will establish realistic expectations of the benefits and results of their services.

- Members will treat all client information that is not public knowledge as confidential, will prevent it from access by unauthorized people, and will not take advantage of proprietary or privileged information, either for use by them, their firm or another client, without the client's permission.

- Members will avoid conflicts of interest, or the appearance of such, and will disclose to a client any circumstances or interests that might influence their judgment and objectivity.

- Members will refrain from inviting an employee of an active or inactive client to consider alternative employment without prior discussion with the client.

Engagements

- Members will only accept assignments which they possess the expertise to perform, and will only assign staff with the requisite expertise.

- Members will ensure that before accepting any engagement, a mutual understanding of the objectives, scope, work plan, and fee arrangements has been established.

- Members will offer to withdraw from a consulting engagement when their objectivity or integrity may be impaired.

Fees

- Members will agree in advance with a client on the basis for fees and expenses, and will charge fees and expenses that are reasonable, legitimate and commensurate with the services delivered and the responsibility accepted.

- Members will disclose to their clients in advance any fees or commissions that they receive for equipment, supplies or services they could recommend to their clients.

Profession

- Members will respect the individual and corporate rights of clients and consulting colleagues, and will not use proprietary information or methodologies without permission.

- Members will represent the profession with integrity and professionalism in their relations with their clients, colleagues and the general public.

- Members will report violations of this Code to the Institute, and will ensure that other consultants working on behalf of the member abide by this Code.

* * * * *

The Institute of Management Consultants USA, Inc. (IMC USA) adopted its first Code of Ethics in 1968. Since that time IMC USA has modified the wording of the Code for additional clarity and relevance to clients. The current Code was approved February 22, 2002. It is consistent with the International Code of Professional Conduct published by the International Council of Management Consulting Institutes (ICMCI) of which IMC USA is a founding member.

Members who apply for the CMC (Certified Management Consultant) designation must pass a written examination on the application of the IMC USA Code of Ethics to client service. The CMC mark is awarded to consultants who have met high standards of education, experience, competence and professionalism.

Appendix E

Advice From the Experts

Throughout this book I've drawn on and referenced interviews and input from a number of senior executives, consultants, former consultants, entrepreneurs, and other "experts." For those of you who want a more comprehensive look at what they had to say in the context of our interviews, here are relevant excerpts from some of our sessions. For ease of reading and to remove a lot of redundancy, I've edited and combined them into what reads like a single, focused group discussion, though the interviews were actually conducted independently and combined afterward. (And not all respondents were asked exactly the same questions).

Participants included eight individuals with backgrounds in a broad range of different industries – healthcare, publishing, media/telecommunications, computer hardware/software, consumer packaged goods, industrial products, business services, etc. And they have different functional expertise – sales, marketing, information technology, operations/manufacturing, human resources, customer service, etc. Three of the participants also hold or held very senior general management positions — EVP or CEO – and have worked closely with consultants as the key client contact.

Seven of them live and work in the United States; one (an American citizen) has lived and worked overseas for the last several years (and insists the key issues are exactly the same there as here). A couple of them are former teachers and academics as well. Two are female, the other six are male.

The thing they all have in common is that they are, or have been, consultants. As you'll see, that makes them more alike than different from each other in many ways.

One additional comment or observation: Throughout the book I've tried very hard to stick to the actual work of consulting, not the entrepreneurial aspects of setting up and running a consulting business. In the course of the interviews with consultants, however, many of the administrative, business, and personal issues came to the surface as being even more important than those of the actual work of consultants. You're bound to notice these references in the discussion that follows. I've intentionally left them in because I think they provide an important added dimension to the consideration of whether or not to consult.

Those of you who are seriously considering your own "lone-wolf" consulting business would be well advised to take both kinds of issues into account.

The Discussion

Goodman: Let's start with how you decided to become a consultant. Was it a considered decision, or was it more opportunistic? Did you have a project in hand or did you have to beat the bushes? What issues did you consider?

> **Carlos:** For me the driving force was necessity! I was with a company that closed its doors when no further funding was possible due to the economy. After spending twenty-three years with just two companies in both management and sales, it became necessary to evaluate what to do with the rest of my life.
>
> I had no original plans to be a consultant, but fortunately a number of acquaintances kept recommending me, and inquiries started coming in. I also did my own "urgent" mailings and received a remarkable 30 replies out of 200 letters. I whittled that down to three very likely clients, did

the research on each and made my presentations. I actually surprised myself and landed all three!

It was simple what issues to consider: Money or no money.

Rob: Hunger was the driving force behind the formation of my consulting business. A change in politics and policy saw the drying up of research grants and university teaching positions. I just didn't have any good alternatives.

Susan: I kind of stumbled into consulting. When I lost my job [due to a reduction in force] a friend asked if I could help her out on a temporary basis. Since I didn't have anything better to do just then, I said I would. That was the start of a very nice second career for me.

Tom (who had two separate stints as a consultant before going back to a senior management position): Originally I joined a large consulting firm as a way-station between corporate jobs. They had the clients and infrastructure; I was the client contact/consultant. Eventually, though, I found the corporate job I wanted – or thought I wanted – and returned to corporate life.

Another time, several years later, I was working in San Francisco and I needed to stay there for family reasons when the company moved. Another firm in the [San Francisco] Bay Area approached me with a long-term consulting offer – a guarantee of one year, a bonus incentive, and some pretty attractive extras. Since I had previously consulted, it seemed like a good solution to my problem, and it gave me the foundation to find other consulting work. After a while, when I was ready and able to relocate, I gave up consulting again and went back to the client side.

Martin: I had been thinking of being a consultant for a long time and had actually given it a lot of thought, so the decision to begin my own practice was a very considered one.

I didn't have a project in hand when I started, but I got some good advice from a friend that I'm really glad I followed. Too often new consultants hang out their shingle mistakenly thinking clients will show up in droves. Of course, the odds are against that happening.

What I decided to do is work initially through other consulting companies [as an independent sub-contractor]. Though I made a little less on each project, it provided me with important experience and credibility. Now I still work as an independent contractor for other consulting companies, but I also serve a number of my own clients directly.

Andy: I had thought about my own business for a number of years, so in that sense it was a considered decision. At first, I only looked at opportunities that were within my comfort zone … in the same industry where I'd spent the previous twenty-one years of my working career. Then one day I asked myself, "How do people really decide what they would like to do, and how do they identify career options where they have a good chance of success?"

My questions led me to a consulting company that helps people determine their goals, needs, and expectations prior to going into their own business. I went through their process, looked at three other businesses, and determined that

I enjoy coaching, mentoring, and developing talent – and I like helping people. The upshot is that I joined that company as an independent consultant – essentially owning my own franchise and running my own business.

The issues I considered were financial, concern about losing face-to-face contact with people [since most of the interaction with clients is via telephone], and the challenge of a new kind of career.

Alan: I worked with a consultant when I was at [a client company], and I always thought consulting looked like a wonderful way to live. The lifestyle was appealing, and I knew the fees were very attractive. So when I lost my job in a corporate consolidation, I was really eager to try my hand at consulting, and I did. That's how I got started.

Goodman: What attracted you to consulting?

Carlos (who has a law degree but has never practiced): What attracted me to consulting? Money, dignity, self-esteem, respect, and control of my life. How else could I start a business with very little operating capital, be a chief executive, be paid $250 an hour (or more), establish credentials, and work less than five days a week. When I looked at it that way, it was an easy decision. After all, earning multi-six-figures working four days a week beats opening a law office and working eighty-plus hours a week while needing at least five years to build a practice.

Tom: What attracted me to consulting was an opportunity to see other businesses, to contribute, but not to have to make a long-term commitment right away. Also, to some degree, there was time management flexibility, and that looked pretty attractive to me.

Carol: I was really turned off by the politics and back-stabbing in [my former company] and the corporate world generally. I also felt that as a woman I might not have the same opportunities for promotion and senior management responsibility. Consulting seemed like a viable alternative to me, so I made the leap when I had the chance. I guess I was escaping from a greater evil, not really attracted to consulting per se.

Andy: What attracted me most was the opportunity to control my own destiny. Of course, I also like the autonomy that consulting gives me. And, since I am working with many different clients, there is variety in my day.

Alan: The lifestyle was the main thing. I had young children then, and I wanted to have some time with them. I thought consulting would let me set my own schedule so I could integrate my work and my family life.

Goodman: *What were the biggest negatives?*

Carlos: The negatives came roaring into the limelight pretty quickly. Let's start with the fact that everyone saw me as the Grim Reaper. I was cast instantly into the persona of the "headcount" specialist. Everyone wanted to tell me how indispensable they were, what jerks all the others were, and how the company was "all screwed up." I was somewhere between the company shrink and the executioner. And that wasn't exactly what I had in mind for myself.

Maybe the biggest negative, though, was Uncle Sam, Aunt State and Local brethren. You know who I mean – the tax authorities. You want to see taxed? Then start your own consulting business and discover the 15% self-employment tax, the other assessments and limitations, and figure that you'll walk away with less than half of what you billed! Now that certainly doesn't sound so good, does it? And then you have to consider that no one but you is providing for your retirement, covering your health benefits, and did I mention insurance?

There is a price for independence and self-esteem.

Tom: The negatives are many. For starters, it's hard to prospect while you are delivering the consulting. That's a constant problem. Then there's little sense of being part of the team, and sometimes you have to take assignments you don't like just to keep the business going.

And there can be lulls where you have inadequate business, but you aren't comfortable going on vacation for fear of missing an assignment. Conversely, when you are very busy you can't take a vacation either.

Finally, there are few friends – consulting is a very lonely business.

Martin: I don't know if you'd consider it a negative, but I've found that I have to continually remind myself about the importance of marketing and self-promotion while working on a full-time project. This is especially critical for me as a solo practitioner. It's very easy to forget about marketing when you get caught up in the exuberance of an interesting and financially rewarding assignment.

Andy: I expected that it would take some time to get the business going, but it has taken a little longer than expected. So that has been a negative ... or at least a hurdle.

I have found it difficult to not concentrate on the money – or lack of it. Other than that it is mostly as expected since I spoke to a lot of other consultants prior to making my decision.

Alan: The negative that really got me was how hard the work was and how many unproductive hours I spent on airplanes, in airports, in hotels, in rental car lines – all away from home. When I wasn't jumping through hoops for my client I was looking for more work. There was never a time when I was able to really relax.

Goodman: Were there any surprises after you began consulting?

Rob (who consulted on his own for a while, then joined a large consulting firm): You bet! The biggest surprise – and the worst surprise – was the amount of selling involved in the process. And I don't mean just finding clients. The effort and time required to evaluate, cost, and design a project, and then present it to the potential client, were not only surprises but major factors in my seeking employment with a larger company.

Carol: I think I was most surprised by the pressure. I always try to do the best for my clients, to give them 110% all the time. In that sense, I create a lot of my own pressure. But then I also feel guilty if I'm not spending at least a day or two each week prospecting for my next job or my next client. When you put those together, it's a very pressure-filled job.

Appendix E: Advice From the Experts

Alan: I was surprised by how hard it was to juggle everything and make it all come out right. I spent six or seven hours a week on admin – running my business, catching up on bookkeeping, opening mail ... that kind of stuff. And nobody was paying me for that time. I almost felt guilty breaking for lunch because I should have been prospecting for another project, or calling a client to make sure a current project was on track.

Susan: The surprise for me is how much I enjoy consulting. I get to do all the things I like and don't have to put up with the corporate B.S. any more.

Goodman: Did you go into consulting expecting it to be a permanent/ long-term thing, or was it always viewed as an interim job?

Carlos (who consulted successfully for about a year, but is now looking for a full-time client-side position): When I started consulting, I had no idea if it would be an interim deal or possibly a new career. Of course, I hoped it would be just the answer to my prayer for independence.

Tom: I always saw it as an interim thing. I wasn't sure for how long or exactly how it would work out, but I never saw myself as a consultant forever.

Susan: I viewed it as a temporary thing when I began, but it worked out so well I've continued as a consultant for eight years now.

Andy: The decision was planned as permanent; I did not view it as an interim thing. I was very concerned that at my age [early 50s] and with my previous industry experience it would be difficult to replicate my previous responsibilities and income. I feel that there is both age and income discrimination that is difficult to overcome.

Carol: I don't know that I really expected either outcome when I started. I wanted my consulting business to be successful, but I never closed the door to going back to the client side if the right thing came along. As it happens, I now enjoy what I'm doing so much that I can't imagine doing anything else, and I doubt there's another job out there that I'd take under any circumstance.

Alan: I went into consulting expecting it to be my career until retirement. It didn't take long, though, for me to change that fantasy! It wasn't the lifestyle I had anticipated.

Goodman: Some of you consulted for a while then went back to the client-side — or you're thinking of doing so. Why?

Carlos: Well, I haven't returned to the dark side yet, but I can hope. Seriously, the responsibilities in being a sole entrepreneur are interesting with some great benefits. The downside is that you still must pay the taxes, work the hours, fill the pipeline, and make your own contributions to retirement and benefits. The biggest plus is the ability to control your life and maybe improve your golf game too. But, the negative aspects are strong too. In this economy, no one is beating down doors to hire the best consultant full-time, forever, until death do us part.

Tom: I went back to the client side because that was where I felt most comfortable. It was not a surprise; I always saw consulting as a temporary, stop-gap way to feed my family and remain plugged in to the business community.

Alan: I went back to the client-side to save my sanity and my marriage. I wasn't cut out to be a consultant, and I wasn't smart enough to figure that out before I became one.

Goodman: What are the qualities or skills you think are required for a person to be successful and happy as a consultant? Are some more important than others?

Carlos: There are a bunch of skills and personal qualities you need to have if you want to be successful as a consultant. The ones that come to mind immediately are:

- the ability to work alone and feel alone,
- the ability to sort out fact from fiction,
- a real understanding of business and politics,
- the ability to keep books and aggressively collect accounts payable,
- a "big picture" view of the world ... a visionary,
- the ability to build a plan, focus, communicate your direction,
- the ability to build consensus ... you better be able to sell or it fails,
- sufficient capital to endure the dry spells ... a one-year reserve minimum,
- organization and self discipline to set goals and commitment to exceeding them,
- a strong network of personal contacts,
- excellent references from all of your prior lives,

- family support … emotional, but money wouldn't hurt either,
- friends who care and are interested in how you are doing, and
- a hobby to relieve the stress (unless it leads to more stress).

I would say that I've been very fortunate to have almost all of these, but that still doesn't make it easy when a client fails to pay or when you see a wonderful reference deteriorate due to collection problems.

Andy: I think you need to be able to work on your own, without the benefit of a safety net. You also need to be self-motivated and be a people person. And you need to be able to balance working with present customers as well as finding new ones. These are all critical to success.

Carol: I think people skills are the most important, but that may depend on the kind of consulting you do. You have to be a good listener, be able to interpret what the client is telling you, and present your recommendations in a way that will ensure client support and acceptance. Those, at least in my view, are people skills. The other thing you need is a fertile, creative mind that can come up with out-side-the-box answers and approaches. That's really what consulting is all about, isn't it?

Rob: The ability to assimilate information very quickly is the big requirement. If you can do that, you can really do anything. You also need the type of personality that can make important decisions alone, quickly and with a high percentage of correct analyses and choices, without burning out or going mad. And definitely the love of sales and selling.

Susan: Gee, I'm not sure I can enumerate all the requirements. Probably the most important are excellent communication skills. You have to gather information effectively and efficiently, and you have to deliver it the same way. That means you have to read your audience, use the right words and body language, explain yourself clearly, and – well – be a great communicator.

Tom: I can think of a number of qualities and skills. The really important ones are self-confidence, good personal interactive skills, good listening skills, genuine creativity, a significant base of experience from which to draw, good writing skills, and good, enthusiastic presentation skills. These are absolutely MANDATORY.

There are a number of other things that are important, but not to the same degree. For example, you really should have analytic/quantitative skills, social skills, good empathy, good interpretive skills (in order to figure out what the client really means), a hunger for delivering high quality work (or to be driven by a fear of failure), intellectual curiosity, a good sense of humor, and good story-telling ability.

And as I consider the lists of mandatory and other important requirements, I don't think you can be deficient in any of them.

Martin: I suppose it depends a little on what kind of consulting you plan to do. For me, the important requirements would be a solid general business background, hands-on-experience in the corporate world, strong analytical and listening skills, a knack for working in partnership with clients in a discovery mode rather than having all the answers, patience to deal with ambiguity, a penchant for being resourceful, and the ability to synthesize information and present it verbally and in writing.

All of these have proven to be important for me. If I can add a personal observation, though, it's that the ability to write well is really essential for a consultant. So much of the work is leaving a well-documented trail.

Goodman: What advice would you give to someone who is thinking of consulting as a second career? What would you say to someone who wants to consult while between jobs ... to earn a little extra cash, make some contacts, maybe find a great new job, etc.?

Carlos: I'd first ask them if they have the patience, the network, and the money to sustain the effort.

There is nothing wrong with doing something between jobs. After all eating does become a habit most families develop. However, think long and hard about what specialization you really have, how to market it, and what the effects are likely to be for you and your future as a consultant if you become another in the "sweatshop of this economy" who agrees to sew another sleeve on the jacket in four weeks. Being a temp-worker is NOT the same as being a consultant. As a temp-worker you have no power and you get no respect from your employer or your fellow workers. You are simply a temporary make-do worker. That belittles the role of those engaged in real executive management, mentoring, and corporate strategizing.

Appendix E: Advice From the Experts

Tom: I guess I'd start with the suggestion that a would-be consultant should first conduct a very careful assessment of his or her skill set compared to the requisite skill set for a successful consultant. Be honest with yourself, because the result is something you'll have to live with. If you meet all the criteria, and you love variety and can tolerate uncertainty, it may be right for you.

I'd then say that you better remember how hard it is to get new jobs while you're delivering old jobs. If that doesn't scare you, and if you absolutely believe in your abilities, consulting may be right for you.

When I was consulting, I was frustrated by the fact that I could never see my ideas through because the client took the next steps. That was really frustrating for me, and it's probably why I've spent most of my time as a client. If you think you'd be similarly frustrated, don't consult. You'll be just as frustrated as I was.

I also felt that consulting required that I find new problems within a client's business, so I could sell him a new project. I had an ethical problem with that. If that bothers you, don't consult, because selling a new project to a current client is the single easiest way to keep the revenue rolling in. It's a commercial necessity. That works for some people and not for others.

If you do end up consulting, "over-deliver" should be your mantra!

Martin: My advice is this: Money sometimes comes in big chunks and sometimes it doesn't come in at all. You really need to learn to manage cash flow very carefully.

Susan: It worked out well for me, but I don't think I'd recommend it for most people. Consulting is a very lonely life and it requires a lot of stamina, self-confidence, and hard work. I guess my advice would be to talk to as many people as you can find who have done the kind of consulting you would do. Ask them the hard questions and use their experience as input before you make your final decision.

If what you're really thinking is that consulting is strictly a between-jobs endeavor, then it's definitely a bad idea. It will take you longer to set up and develop a real, income-producing venture than it's worth. Spend the time finding your next job instead.

Andy (who consults with would-be entrepreneurs): My advice to others is to think through what you want to accomplish. Are you running away from corporate America or are you running towards self-employment via consulting? Be brutally honest with yourself, and determine whether this is something you want to do long term, or simply a "stop-gap" measure. If you think you'll grab something better when it comes around (in terms of a job), your clients will see this and probably stay away from you.

I know it's a little self-serving since I'm in the business, but anyone who is thinking about an undertaking of their own owes it to themselves to take advantage of what [my company] has learned about the critical success factors and requirements for entrepreneurs, independent consultants, franchise owners, and other go-it-alone ventures. Don't try to do everything on your own; it's almost impossible to be totally objective, and the cost of a wrong decision can be disastrous. We've been there, and we can really help people decide if they're cut out for this [independent] kind of life.

Alan (who went back to the client side about 2 years after becoming a consultant): Be very careful before you choose consulting as a career, and consider what your life will become. Consulting can easily turn into a grinding hourly or per-diem job, no matter how high the pay is. You only earn when you work, and there's no stability or assurance of work in the future. There's no equity or residual income, you're always scrounging for work, and when you ARE working you're at the client's beck and call. The pressures are unbelievable, and you can kiss your family life good-bye. Other than that, it's a lot of fun!

Goodman: Do you know anyone who has successfully used interim consulting as part of his or her job search strategy and then landed a permanent job with the client company?

Carlos: Not really. But many who try consulting as a short-term thing, when they're between jobs, continue as consultants for a long time. There is something addictive about the freedom, the respect, and the money when consulting is going well.

Rob: I know a few people who started out as independent consultants between jobs, did some sub-contracting for a larger consulting firm, and ended up working for the larger firm on a full-time basis. They're still consultants, but they eat more regularly now. I'm not sure that counts, because they didn't go to work for the real client company.

Carol: No, and I think it would be a real mistake for anyone to go into consulting with that possibility as a key reason for their decision.

Alan: No, I don't. I do know a few people, myself included, for whom consulting provided a viable platform for finding the next job, but I don't know anyone who actually got a full-time, permanent position with their client company as a direct result of consulting for them.

Susan: No. I think it's very unlikely that a client would hire a consultant for a full-time job. If they thought they needed a full-time person, why would they hire a consultant in the first place?

Goodman: Any other thoughts or comments about consulting that might be useful?

Carlos: Yes, respect yourself and carry yourself as though you are advising the President of the United States. Dignity and a strong sense of self-worth will go a long way in building the relationship you want with your clients, and getting paid as you wish.

Alan: I have a new respect for good consultants, having now tried [consulting] myself. I know how to take advantage of what they have to offer, and I don't begrudge them their fees. When I find good consultants, I do everything in my power to keep them working on my business. I also realize that when you hire a consultant, it's the individual that counts, not the name of the firm.

Carol: I've always felt that people should do what they love to do and not worry so much about the money. When I started consulting I thought I had found my calling and would do it regardless of how much I made. The good news, of course, is that if you're good at what you do, you can usually make enough money to satisfy both kinds of needs. You need to trust the universe a little, and trust the fact that the money will come if you're doing what you love and what you're good at.

*   *   *   *   *

Editor's final note: We've chosen to use names that are different from the respondents' real names because a few of them specifically requested anonymity. All the comments, however, reflect what a respondent actually said in response to the questions. When an individual participant's responses are not shown, it's either because he or she wasn't asked that question or the response was so close to another's response as to be redundant.

What people have said about
The Potato Chip Difference

"The Potato Chip Difference *is an informative and easy to read guide that offers lots of good suggestions and tools that you will want to spend time absorbing and using. I recommend this book because it focuses on the planning phase of the self-marketing effort — when you determine the strategy that will guide everything else you do. This is often the most neglected phase of the job search process because so many of us want to jumpstart our searches by pushing resumes out the door so that the phone starts to ring. Take time to make a difference in your search. Read this book and put it to use. It will make a difference for you.*"

Ellen Stuhlmann, Managing Director
ExecuNet's Executive Insider Newsletter

* * * * *

"The Potato Chip Difference *is for you if you want to spend some time learning new tools to better understand yourself, as well as better prepare you to find — and land — that ideal job with the ideal employer. ... The job search is all about using marketing skills to better position, present, and sell yourself to potential employers — and this book will make you better prepared for your next job search.*"

Dr. Randall S. Hansen, Ph.D.
QuintessentialCareers.com

* * * * *

"With all the 'help' out there for job seekers — books, websites, career coaches, you name it — most people need a good road map. The Potato Chip Difference *is an excellent 'first read' for a job seeker.*"

Matthew Sitelman, Senior Vice President
6 Figure Jobs (www.6figurejobs.com)

"The Potato Chip Difference *clearly presents the highly useful application of sound marketing strategy to the job search process, enabling job seekers to better position and differentiate themselves. Because of its clear strategic guidance, the book is particularly useful in the early stages of a job search.*"

T. W. O'Neal
Senior Vice President, IMG

* * * * *

"*In the executive search business we see the wisdom of Goodman's advice almost daily. We work exclusively with marketing people. These are senior-level executives who wouldn't dream of creating a marketing plan without first developing a well-conceived marketing strategy. Yet when it comes to their own professional career too often they seem to ignore career strategy in pursuit of off-target short-term "opportunities." The result of this oversight is an unfocused career path with too many unexplainable job changes.*"

John Bissell, Managing Partner
Gundersen Partners, L.L.C.

* * * * *

"*Goodman's* The Potato Chip Difference *is a valuable tool for anyone thinking about or looking for a new job. His unique contribution (as a marketing consultant) is guidance through the self-positioning process: How to recognize, evaluate, and organize your talents so as to highlight them in the mind of an employer ... and to get the job you deserve!*"

Akasha Ames, President
The Snowdon Group

About the Author

Michael A. Goodman is a veteran marketing/ management consultant with expereince in and exposure to a wide spectrum of business situations and marketing applications.

Before beginning his own career as a consultant, Goodman held senior marketing management positions at Procter & Gamble, Frito-Lay, and International Playtex. Since then, the list of clients he has served reads like a who's who of well-known global corporations across a broad range of industries – from high-tech, low-tech and no-tech products to healthcare, travel, and financial services, food and beverages, health, beauty, medical, and household products, industrial chemicals, fashion apparel, publishing, and a host of other business-to-business, consumer packaged goods, and non-traditional marketing challenges.

In his previous book, *The Potato Chip Difference: How to apply leading edge marketing strategies to landing the job you want*, Goodman applied the same strategic approach to job seeking and career planning that top management consulting firms use with major clients. In this book, *Rasputin For Hire*, he offers insights and advice for those considering management consulting between jobs or as a second career.